My Biggest Mistake

My Biggest Mistake

Edited by
Roger Trapp

Published in Association with the *Independent on Sunday*

BUTTERWORTH
HEINEMANN

THE INDEPENDENT
ON SUNDAY

Butterworth-Heinemann Ltd
Linacre House, Jordan Hill, Oxford OX2 8DP

℞ A member of the Reed Elsener group

OXFORD LONDON BOSTON
MUNICH NEW DELHI SINGAPORE SYDNEY
TOKYO TORONTO WELLINGTON

First published 1993
Reprinted 1993

British Library Cataloguing in Publication Data
My Biggest Mistake
  I. Trapp, Roger
  658.4

ISBN 0 7506 0859 5

Composition by Genesis Typesetting, Laser Quay, Rochester, Kent
Printed in England by Clays Ltd, St Ives plc

Contents

Part Three Financial Mistakes   171

Part Four Miscellaneous Mistakes   199

Index of names   215

Preface

The 'My Biggest Mistake' feature is as old as the *Independent on Sunday*. When the newspaper was launched on 28 January 1990, its pages included the first in a series of business figures' blunders.

Virgin founder Richard Branson's admission that he had stayed with his original bank for longer than was good for his growing company set the ball rolling, and in the weeks ahead the likes of Gerald Ratner, the jewellery retailer; Sir Gordon Borrie, the former Director General of Fair Trading, and Sir John Harvey-Jones, the ex-chairman of ICI, entered the confessional.

The idea was dreamed up as senior Newspaper Publishing staff were planning a business section that would be entertaining as well as authoritative – in other words, different from the established competition in more ways than its tabloid form.

Developed by the section's first editor, Peter Wilson-Smith, and Anne Ferguson, who originally took charge of the Inside Business pages in which it appears, 'My Biggest Mistake' quickly struck a chord with readers.

Part of the appeal is no doubt the joy of seeing familiar and supposedly successful figures owning up to errors of judgement and other varying degrees of mistake. But there is a more serious side.

Some of the well over 100 contributors have confessed to fairly trifling incidents and then sought to show how they then turned these into their greatest triumphs. Others have sought to say that their mistake was not to appreciate the capacity of others to make mistakes. But the majority have displayed so much candour that not only have those involved hopefully learned from their mistakes but so also have their readers. Competitors have even been known to express surprise at the readiness to make such admissions.

And while prominent executives like those above have made up a significant proportion of the contributors, there have also been offerings from the not so famous, whose experiences might be expected to be more in tune with those of the average owner-manager reading the newspaper in the hope of picking up some tips. Indeed, some of the most instructive mistakes have been made by individuals and companies that are some way short of household names.

For instance, Stephen Franklin of the UK division of Commodore Business Machines says that his biggest mistake was trying to sell home computer packages containing products not related to computers. The error was to try to catch on to the 'flavour of the month' rather than ask whether it was what the customer wanted. The lesson that he learned the hard way – 'Just because everybody is jumping on the bandwagon of a new promotion scheme don't automatically assume it will work for you' – is particularly true of markets like home computers, but it applies to many other areas of business, too.

In the same way, Angus Rankine of the corporate clothing designer Jacqueline de Baer claims his biggest mistake occurred when he gave too large a contract to one supplier while running the marketing department at Canary Wharf. This project may yet figure in many biggest mistakes of the future, but this particular setback – and the lesson learned – are not peculiar to it. Many people will be able to relate to his new-found fear of putting too many eggs in one basket and might take note of his formula for avoiding it.

But that does not mean that the contributions from the likes of Sir John Harvey-Jones have no value beyond the voyeuristic. First, it is encouraging to discover that even those who follow a spell at the helm of one of Britain's most prestigious companies by becoming a business pundit make mistakes. Second, these figures were not always at the top.

In fact, some of their mistakes were committed while they were junior employees. As such, they could could hardly be classed as major errors of strategy. But they could have nipped promising careers in the bud. Consequently, there are lessons to be learned. By the employee: 'He/she did something like I have just done and survived to become a success.' By the employer: 'Do not be quick to write off staff. Today's idiot may turn out to be tomorrow's captain of industry.'

Take Brian MacMahon, for instance. As he says, the two vital attributes for a career in the pensions industry are reliability and trustworthiness. So, when just before his wedding day he managed to throw both to the wind by neglecting to renew the life assurance policy of an important client of his employer he naturally assumed the worst. It took an understanding employer to keep him on. But MacMahon's took the view that the experience would ensure that he never forgot the importance of those two attributes, and that chastened young man went on to become chairman of the National Association of Pension Funds.

Likewise, Sir Christopher Harding found himself in trouble while a graduate trainee at ICI (the scene of tribulations for one or two other contributors). Having on one occasion failed to make appropriate travel arrangements for an important conference, he says he learned the importance of attending to detail, and has gone on to be chairman of British Nuclear Fuels and the services group BET.

As should by now be obvious, the 100 or so contributions gathered together for this collection cover a wide range of personalities.

Some continue to go from strength to strength. Others have had their difficulties. These may have been before the article appeared. This was the case with Sophie Mirman, who was able to reflect on what had brought down Sock Shop from the vantage point of a new venture, and with Swraj Paul, whose mistake is enshrined in UK company law as the Caparo case. Or the problems may have arrived subsequently, as with George Walker, who – following a lengthy and expensive restructuring operation – is no longer associated with the company that bears his name, and Nik Powell, whose film company Palace Group has run into financial trouble.

The feature has also covered the whole spectrum of business, from the traditional industries, such as steel and manufacturing, through retail to the new, such as computers, marketing and media.

Nor has it been limited to the boss class. Beside the captains of industry, the senior managers and the entrepreneurs, for instance, stand the representatives of their former adversaries, the trade unions. Since both AEU leader Bill Jordan and Peugeot Talbot managing director Geoff Whalen draw on their time at what was once known as British Leyland for their mistakes, this is particularly informative.

There are also politicians of varying hues who have worked in business or finance, plus the odd orchestra manager and charity organizer. In fact, anybody who runs something qualifies.

Just one group is notable by its absence: a small but significant band of managers who instructed their staff to say that they never made mistakes. They know who they are; with luck, they will at least learn something from the failings of others.

But for all the variety of contributors, there are distinct themes running through their experiences. In what is perhaps further support for the view that the differences between various types of business are often exaggerated, the mistakes gathered here for the most part fall broadly into one of three categories – strategic (by some margin, the largest), personnel and financial. As a result, they have been divided into sections under these headings.

Just as there are some that could be said to span at least two if not all three categories, there are others that defy such easy classification. Since some of these are too interesting, entertaining or informative to lose, a further miscellaneous section will close the book.

Finally, an explanatory note. Several of the people featured in the following pages are no longer doing the jobs attributed to them in the biographies accompanying their mistakes. While some have moved on or retired of their own free will, others – such as those referred to above – have fallen victim to the tough economic conditions that have prevailed throughout the life of the *Independent on Sunday* – and the 'My Biggest Mistake' column. Where appropriate, their changes of circumstances is noted in the introductory text.

Roger Trapp

Acknowledgements

My greatest debt goes to those from a variety of walks of business life who agreed to bare their souls in public – and open themselves up to ridicule from friends and competitors alike. Without them, the 'My Biggest Mistake' column would have been just a gleam in an editor's eye.

I am also grateful to all the past and present members of the staff of the *Independent* and *Independent on Sunday* who found the time to persuade often reluctant executives to admit to blunders, and to the outside contributors – particularly Corinne Simcock, Philip Stein and Malcolm Wheatley – who have helped keep the feature entertaining, informative and, above all, alive.

Part One
Strategic Mistakes

Strategy is one of today's management 'buzz words'. It crops up alongside others, such as quality and service, whenever senior executives or, more often, consultants are trying to put across some vision of a company's future.

Here, though, it is used in its wide sense to encompass any mistakes that relate to the direction or objectives of an organization.

As a result, it extends from such basic blunders as Lord Delfont's turning down the chance to manage the Beatles, through various permutations of expansion into unknown areas, to such monumental episodes as Lord Rees-Mogg's decision to agree to a shutdown of *The Times* without having a Wapping-style solution at hand.

This being the 1990s, there are in the following pages several rueful descriptions of 1980s' deals and developments gone sour. The United States has proved a particular stumbling block, with Roger Saul of clothing and luggage company Mulberry, Sophie Mirman of Sock Shop and Chris Wright of Chrysalis Records all in one way or another finding the American Dream turning into a nightmare.

The fact that expanding into a country that is apparently one big market populated by people speaking in an approximation of English is more complicated than it looks is now well known. As such, the subject is the basis of many business school courses. But for Roger Saul, Sophie Mirman and Chris Wright the experience was no case study. They learned the hard way and at great cost. Their insights are of great use to anybody who might be tempted to, in the words of Roger Saul, fall for the American Dream.

Gerald Ratner's mistake is also connected with the allure of the New World. Only his regret is letting a deal fall through his fingers rather than making one that turned bad. Given his recent troubles, though, it is doubtful whether he holds the same view now.

But no matter what is said or written, America will continue to exert a strong pull on this side of the Atlantic. Dan Wagner, for instance, is convinced that his Market Analysis and Information Database – an on-line marketing intelligence and data retrieval service – would have taken off much sooner had he launched it in the United States rather than Britain.

The flavour of the times also comes over in such contributions as TUC general secretary Norman Willis's realization that he had not paid sufficient attention to women's representation and in Scottish Provident managing director David Woods' admission that he tried to rush a corporate culture change.

Others are more timeless, though no less valuable for that. For example, Sir Hector (now Lord) Laing admits that at one time United Biscuits put all its energies into marketing and turned its back on its traditional strength of production. Marketing also played a part in the development of George Bull, who has moved to the foods side of Grand Metropolitan after a lengthy spell in the drinks business. In the latter, he learned that, while select brands should not be cheapened through overexposure, no amount of expenditure on a product will persuade consumers to buy it unless it is good. Meanwhile, Lord Marsh confesses that when he was in at the beginning of TV-am he succumbed to what he himself calls 'one of the commonest clichés in the business world' – the idea that a particular venture is sufficiently different from all others to require a special approach to its running.

The thing about mistakes is that with few exceptions they are only recognized with the benefit of hindsight. However, time does not stand still. So what starts off appearing to be a sound decision can become a mistake, only to seem well founded again when circumstances change.

Take, for instance, Sir Peter Thompson's gallant admission that he was saved by non-executive directors from leaving National Carriers out of the privatization of what used to be known as National Feight Corporation. Part of his reasoning was that the National Carriers goods yards had turned out to be valuable property sites. But that was in early 1990, before the property market tumbled.

In other words, what seems like a good idea at one time will not necessarily appear that way later. But further down the road it may once again look wise.

Such mistakes can occur in all kinds of organizations, from the very small to the very large – even governments, as Sir Graham Day found when he agreed to take over the helm of what was to become British Shipbuilders. The difference is that, while comparatively minor strategic errors can lead to disaster at small operations, only the truly serious will bring down their larger counterparts.

It is for this reason that Sir John Harvey-Jones, for instance, was able to delay pulling out of a business that was not working out for ICI. As he says, 'Staying overlong in oil was not a disaster in terms of having lost ICI's shirt or anything like that. But it was bad news, and because of my emotional attachment we undoubtedly diverted money into the oil business which wasn't really enough for oil prospecting, but would have been useful in developing other businesses.'

John Leftwich

John Leftwich, 37, is director of marketing for Microsoft Ltd, the UK subsidiary of Microsoft Corporation of the US, the world's leading software company. After receiving a degree in electrical engineering and electronics from Manchester University, he started work for the National Computing Centre. He left in 1980 to go into marketing and three years later joined Apricot Computers, where he rose from publicity manager to group marketing director. He left in 1988 to become director of marketing at Apple Computer UK, from where he was recruited by Microsoft.

I believe my biggest mistake was a classic case of too little foresight. In hindsight, it is easy to see where I went wrong.

Go back almost ten years, and the supremacy now enjoyed by personal computers that are IBM-compatible was far from evident. In fact, I think I'm right in saying that the UK was the last major marketplace where IBM became the market leader.

At the time I was group marketing director of Apricot Computers, and the office computer business was fragmented, to say the least. We were slogging it out with a host of competitors – IBM, of course, but also Apple, Commodore, Olivetti and others. We knew the key to success lay in making our computers compatible with those of another company – but which one? For a variety of reasons, we decided to make the Apricot PC compatible with the Sirius PC from Victor.

The Sirius was designed by Chuck Peddle, the American who came up with the Commodore PET, and was frankly better than IBM's offering at the time, although not dissimilar. So we thought it would win out in the end. Our Sirius-compatible Apricot was a big success: we achieved market leadership and had an installed base of 50,000 or so customers, and in 1984 we decided that the time had come to launch the Apricot PC on the US market. I went over to the States for six months to try to get things moving.

It was a salutary experience. I was 28 and still relatively wet behind the ears, I suppose. But as the six months passed, it became increasingly obvious that the IBM-compatible standard was gaining ground and would ultimately dominate the market. Our machine was almost compatible – 95 per cent or so – but not compatible enough. It would run products like Lotus 1–2–3 – but only after we had paid the software companies huge 'porting' fees to write a version for our computer. I realized the Sirius-compatible Apricot was doomed, but back here it proved a difficult message to get across.

Privately, I was convinced, but we had a strong commitment to our existing customers who would lose out if we abandoned the current product. And we all know what can happen to the messenger. But barely a matter of months later, the ultimate inevitability had become apparent. So one sunny day in June 1985 we sat down and decided we would launch one more 'old' Apricot PC, but secretly start development of a fully IBM-compatible model.

The problem was we were almost too late: had we acted upon my return from the US, we would have had more room to manoeuvre. Now our backs were against the wall. The following six months were the toughest of my career.

The secret was known only to a few. We had to keep it quiet for fear the uncertainty would result in customers, suppliers and software developers deserting in droves. And we succeeded – but at a cost. When the announcement came, the bottom fell out of the demand for the old Apricots, and we had to write off a £15m inventory – an enormous financial blow for a £90m company. We also had to make redundant 200 or so of our 700 employees. I regard making people redundant as the ultimate management failure.

Overall, I think I learned two lessons: to try to listen to my instincts more, and – perhaps of even greater significance – a resolve to push senior management harder in terms of getting my view across.

31 May 1992

Sir John Harvey-Jones

SIR John Harvey-Jones, 66, began his career in the Royal Navy, interpreting Russian and German. He joined Imperial Chemical Industries at 32, and was appointed chairman in 1982. Noted for his outspoken views and loud ties, Sir John has – since his retirement in 1987 – published a book, *Making it Happen* and presented BBC2's *Troubleshooter.* He divides his time between charities, education, business, public speaking and chairing *The Economist.*

My biggest mistake was holding on to a business longer than I should have done. The attachment started early in my industrial career, which I began with ICI in 1956 when I was 32.

One of my first responsibilities with ICI was the supply of raw materials to the petrochemical business. In 1960 there was a very narrow market in naphtha, which comes from the light fraction of refined oil, and we felt we were being held to ransom by the oil companies which supplied it. As a very junior member of the company, I had been asked to study the market and I suggested we should build our own oil refinery.

So I was in at the birth of the oil business for ICI in the early 1960s. The reasons for going in appeared strategically sound. Our major competitors in the petrochemicals business were the oil companies, which also produced the naphtha we bought. They were in a position to choose where they took the value in the production chain, at our expense. So, in 1960 we decided to go into the oil refining business to maintain the independence of ICI's chemical business.

With the opening up of the North Sea, we started looking for our own oil in partnership with others. In 1974 a consortium we were in with Chevron hit a very large field of which we had a significant share. That led us to believe that the oil business was a good business to be in in its own right, and we set up a business designed to continue prospecting for oil.

Once you've found the oil, extraction and production can be highly profitable and produce lots of cash. In fact, for some years earnings from oil were critical to ICI's performance. When I took over as chairman in 1982 oil represented over half the profits we made. But a field only has a finite life and it was costing us a great deal to keep looking for more. Even when you find another field the payback is not immediate.

Looking for oil was a bit like a drug. I'd been in it from the beginning and I had an emotional attachment to the business. But I kept thinking long and hard about it and eventually had to conclude that in the sort of business ICI is in you plant an acorn and hopefully it grows a tree, which drops more acorns and that's how you develop the business. In oil there's no correlation between having one successful oil strike and growing a forest.

So finally, in 1987, we merged our oil business with Enterprise Oil. Staying overlong in oil was not a disaster in terms of having lost ICI's shirt or anything like that. But it was bad news, and because of my emotional attachment we undoubtedly diverted money into the oil business which wasn't really enough for oil prospecting, but would have been useful in developing other businesses.

In business terms I learned three lessons. First, beware of the allure and attraction of your own creation. Second, be very, very clear about the cash-generative characteristics of the business you're in as well as the profit. Third, and the most difficult, it pays you to take decisions sooner rather than waiting until they're forced upon you.

There's another lesson, too. In those days business theory was in favour of vertical integration. That was largely because companies were able to measure the benefits, but they couldn't measure the risks. It was only from the early 1980s that everyone realized that vertical integration means putting most of the capital behind the front end of the business, which has the highest risk.

13 May 1990

Ian Hay Davison

Ian Hay Davison, 58, was educated at Dulwich College and the London School of Economics. He was managing partner of Arthur Andersen from 1966 to 1982 and chaired the UK Accounting Standards Committee from 1982 to 1984. In 1983, he took on the cleaning up of Lloyd's of London, which had been rocked by a series of scandals, an experience that he described in his book, *A View of the Room*. In 1987, he chaired the Hong Kong Securities Review Committee, which looked at the Hong Kong securities market. He is chairman of Laing & Cruickshank, the broker owned by Crédit Lyonnais, and a director of Newspaper Publishing, which publishes *The Independent on Sunday*.

The biggest business mistake I have been involved in involved inflation accounting.

I was chairman of the Accounting Standards Committee from 1982 to 1984, and it was during my reign that inflation accounting was really given its death blow. The question is how the devil we ever got into that situation.

Whenever inflation emerges as a problem in this country the accountants get interested because accounts do not tell the truth about what is happening to costs.

There was a problem in the 1940s and it happened again in 1970. But this time the accountants were ready for it. They had devised a simple system for adjusting for inflation, called purchase-price accounting, which was on the point of being introduced.

At that point, the Government – in the form of Michael Heseltine – blew the whistle. The Government feared that if you could index accounts, then you could also index gilts. It was the view of the Heath government then that the effect of indexing debt, or gilts, or securities would be to make inflation too comfortable to live with. Then it would become a permanent part of the scene.

So in 1975 the Government set up the Sandilands Committee, which came up with current-cost accounting. This adjusts the accounts, not by price indices, but by estimates of current values, which is inherently much more subjective. Foolishly, the accountants fell into the Government's trap and agreed to introduce an accounting system based on current-cost accounting. At that point, I was a member of Sir Douglas Morpeth's long-suffering and hard-working inflation-accounting committee. We had to define a system of accounting, based on the current-cost accounting recommendation of the Sandilands Committee, that could cope with inflation.

My job was to handle the production of a manual on inflation accounting called for by the Sandilands Report. In fact, the manual was the one part of our work that was an undoubted economic success. It generated £35,000 in royalties and covered one-third of the total cost of committee staff. In those days inflation accounting was big business, at least for publishers.

There was widespread opposition to the subjectivity implicit in current-cost accounting, which led to the production of an extremely watered-down version, known as SSAP16 in 1980. (Rules of the Accounting Standards Committee are known as Statements of Standard Accounting Practice – SSAPs.) Even this was eventually rejected.

However, even before all this wonderful work was ready to be used, Mrs Thatcher came to power, and adopted a tactic which none of us could have foreseen. She dealt with accounting for inflation by abolishing inflation. But when, in 1982, it became my turn to chair the Accounting Standards Committee, the top rule-making body, inflation accounting was still on the agenda. We'd been at it for over ten years and the Government was introducing indexed gilts.

My biggest mistake was being part of the profession that was gulled by Mr Heseltine into going along with current-cost accounting, and wasting ten years on failing to come up with a solution. I suppose I should have stood up in 1976 and said we should have nothing to do with this. Now, with inflation once again nearing the 10 per cent mark, analysts are beginning to question the accuracy of historic costs in accounts. But at least this time it isn't my problem.

29 April 1990

Linda Mchugh

Linda McHugh, 42, is chief executive of the Pitman Training Group. On leaving Manchester University she took a diploma in business studies and later an MBA at INSEAD in France. Her career began in marketing in 1971, and by 1979 she was managing director of Graham Kemp Public Relations. In 1982 she became business development manager for AGB Research, the world's fourth-largest market research company. Two years later she became chief executive of Industrial Market Research, a subsidiary, and in 1990 became managing director of AGB Market Information.

My biggest mistake was not having the guts to do a management buyout when I was chief executive of IMR.

IMR had gone through all sorts of changes during its existence and, for various reasons, we decided in 1985 to put the company into voluntary liquidation. The idea was to transfer all the assets into a clean subsidiary without a past, then buy the company back from the liquidator.

Of course, you can't have a pretend liquidation; you have to do it for real. What I hadn't appreciated was that the liquidator would go through the procedure properly, and that meant putting the company up for sale, not just saying to AGB, 'How much will you pay to buy it back?' In those days it was extremely rare to have offered for sale by a liquidator a company that was actually profitable, with a big order book and plenty of clients, so when he advertised in the *Financial Times* we were overwhelmed with potential takers.

I thought, with the folly of inexperience, this meant that sooner or later he would send these people the paperwork, then the company would be sold to AGB anyway. But an awful lot of these people expected to see me, and by the 14th presentation I was getting very fed up with the whole thing. At the same time I had a curious sense of power.

There's no point buying any sort of company if you can't secure the assets – and in this case the assets had two legs and could just walk out of the door. It's not often one has dozens of top businessmen courting one (certainly it's never happened in my private life!), but I realized that these people needed to impress me.

One rainy day I was sitting with our finance director in an Italian restaurant after yet another presentation, and it suddenly occurred to me that if they could buy it, we could buy it. Finance would not be a problem; we could put in a bid ourselves. We got very excited by the prospect of a management buyout and started to put plans into action. Everything was going swimmingly until I had what I took at the time to be an attack of conscience.

I had a great deal of respect for the then chairman of AGB, who had always treated me well, and I felt that buying the company out from under him was somehow dishonourable. I decided not to go through with it, and in the end the company was sold back to AGB. Afterwards, I thought to myself: 'If that was the right thing to do from a moral perspective, how come I feel so bad about it? Where's the consolation of having done the honourable thing?' It just wasn't there.

AGB carried on treating me with absolute fairness, and I was promoted shortly afterwards to a much bigger job. But I got my come-uppance for spinelessness when Robert Maxwell took the company over in 1988. I left two years later, when I couldn't stand it a second longer, but I won't comment further, other than to say that I'm one of those people who lost their pensions.

I certainly regret being too wimpish to go for a management buyout. It's not often that opportunities like that come your way – and this one was really battering at my door.

I'm very happy in my present job; it's much more exciting and has far greater prospects than I would have had with IMR. But the fact remains that when I had the chance, I didn't take it. And that's difficult to live with.

17 May 1992

Geoffrey Deith

Geoffrey Deith, 55, left school at sixteen to become an apprentice engineer. He joined loudspeaker manufacturer R E Ingham in 1963, becoming managing director in 1970. He went on to set up the first single-union, no-strike deal in the UK at the Toshiba TV factory in Plymouth in 1981. He initiated the purchase of Wedgwood by Waterford Glass in 1986, and in December 1987 led a management buyout from Waterford Wedgwood of Aynsley China, where he is currently chief executive.

My biggest mistake was trying to educate the market to buy something it wasn't ready for. I was managing director at R E Ingham, a supplier of wood materials to furniture manufacturers, which was founded by innovator Bob Ingham. We were always looking for a way to add value to our products to improve the business.

We developed a way of putting a PVC covering on wood and then machining it in such a way that furniture manufacturers could make bits of furniture more economically and efficiently.

We identified the loudspeaker as the best use for the technology. These had always been made by attaching four pieces of wood at the corners to make a box, and then varnishing it. By coating a long strip of wood with clear PVC, and then cutting three V-shaped grooves through to the PVC, it could simply be folded to make the casing.

But the time between showing manufacturers the new idea and persuading them to buy it took ages. It was measured in years, not months as we'd expected. There was only one exception, a 68-year old businessman called Noel Fitton, who was running a company called Stereo Sound. He took to it immediately. This encouraged us to invest in capacity in our factory to make the special blanks. But we still could not persuade other loudspeaker manufacturers to buy them. To them it would have meant turning their factories upside down, from assembling and finishing, to taking finished wood and assembling.

This was way before the Zero Defect days of quality management, and they were worried about having to write off anything that was scratched during the manufacturing cycle. We tried to tell them that people who work with delicate materials would be like egg packers – they'd take care not to drop them. But they didn't see it that way. We even went so far as working out for them by how much it would improve their profitability if they used our system. But they wouldn't buy it.

Meanwhile, Noel Fitton was being very, very successful using our blanks. But his business wasn't enough to cover our capital investment and we spent from 1970 to 1972 using management time and huge amounts of money relative to the size of our business. We ran ourselves very, very close to stagnation, but we couldn't make any progress.

Finally, we gave up trying to convince our other customers and decided to use the system ourselves to make our own loudspeakers. We even began installing the electrics and today Ingham is undoubtedly the leading original equipment manufacturer in the UK, supplying speakers to leading brand names, such as Sony and Wharfdale.

The lesson for me was not to underestimate the cost and time it takes to educate a market. It's a nice business school idea to create a market niche and be the one to profit from satisfying it. But creating the niche costs huge amounts of money and an incredible length of time.

Later, when I was running the Rank industrial division, with quite a lot of innovative industrial electronics work, it was valuable to remember that you can be way in front of your time. Yes, the Brits are usually accused of letting other people pinch their ideas, but there is nothing worse than being ahead of your time. It costs a fortune. It's much like running a middle-distance race. You've got to pace yourself. It's no good setting out at a hell of a pace and then wearing yourself out – everyone else just overtakes you.

15 April 1990

Sir Adam Thomson

Sir Adam Thomson was born in 1926 and was educated in Glasgow. In 1944, he joined the Fleet Air Arm, where he trained as a pilot. He co-founded Caledonian Airways in 1961 and became chairman and chief executive in 1964. He was named Businessman of the Year in 1971. He fought a protracted battle against British Airways before British Caledonian was taken over in 1988, the same year that he was appointed chairman of the Institute of Directors. His book, *High Risk*, is published by Sidgwick & Jackson.

About the most important factor in air transport is choosing the right aircraft for the job. This is a very long-term decision since the time between ordering new aircraft and their delivery can be measured in several years. It can even involve placing an order while the aircraft is still on the drawing board.

But in the late 1960s, when we were looking to expand our medium-range fleet, we considered the relative merits of the American Boeing 737 and British Aerospace's BAC 1–11. Our preference was for the former, as its range and capacity were more suitable for our planned operations. The BAC 1–11 was smaller, carried fewer passengers and had an inferior range to the 737.

However, pressure was brought to bear from a number of sources, including the Government to buy British. The leverage to make us do so came in the form of an informal concession we had been given previously which was worth a lot of money to us. To lose it would have been disastrous.

Both manufacturers were offering competitive prices, so that was never an issue. But when it came to a choice between buying British Aerospace and keeping the concession, or buying Boeing and losing it, we put in an order for three BAC 1–11s. Overall, we operated 34 of them.

In November 1970, British Caledonian took over British United Airways, and in doing so acquired a large number of BAC 1–11s. I still favoured the 737 aircraft, but changing the fleet now was not a practical proposition. Once you've got a largish fleet of aircraft it's very expensive to change them; all your pilots are trained on those aeroplanes so there's a big financial penalty in retraining them, and you have hangars full of their equipment.

In the early 1970s there was a big downturn in the industry because of the oil restrictions. By this time the package holiday market was growing fast, with short and medium-haul charter flights taking people to Mediterranean destinations, but it was very competitive, with companies cutting each other's throats and going to the wall. But by 1975–6 it was a much more successful and attractive market and just right for the 737s.

So, once again, I renewed a call for studies on the Boeing 737. Even though I could see it was a better aeroplane for this market, all the studies showed that buying 737s would have a negative impact on the company because of our fleet mix and our resources, which were always in demand for other priorities. Most of our staff were experienced as scheduled flight operators and there was a certain amount of concern among airline staff who, wrongly, I think, felt themselves superior to charter traffic.

Then, too, we didn't look far enough into the future. If we had studied it more closely we would have seen that in ten years' time we'd have been much better off from adding 737s to the fleet. In fact, we could have started a new fleet rather than replacing the current fleet, so as not to interrupt it. But that meant a big investment and we would have had to accept losses for maybe the first three years. But we would have broken even by year four, and spread over ten years, as would have been the case, the benefits would have been considerable.

My biggest mistake was that we never did buy a 737. We should have considered the benefits of investing in Boeing 737 aircraft over a period of five to ten years. Had we taken the bull by the horns then I am certain our profitability would have improved significantly and our cash flow, too. However, there were always other priorities for new scheduled routes, and those won the day.

22 April 1990

Sir Hector Laing

Sir Hector Laing retired as chairman of United Biscuits on his 67th birthday after 45 years spent in his family's business. With an eye to global competitiveness, he tried to merge UB with Imperial, but was seen off by Hanson in 1986 after a ferocious bid battle. A director of the Bank of England, he founded the Per Cent Club which gives corporate money to the community, and serves as joint honorary treasurer of the Conservative Party. Life president of UB, he enjoys flying and gardening.

I joined my company full-time in 1947, after demobilization, and I concentrated my efforts on the production side. As one of the biggest biscuit producers in Europe – we produced 150,000 tons of biscuits at Harlesden in London alone in 1989 – our production expertise has stood us in good stead over the years.

I spent a year each in the factories at Edinburgh and Manchester before settling to manage the Harlesden factory for sixteen years. We became supremely efficient producers of biscuits. But my biggest mistake came when I took my eye off the ball.

In 1965 we brought all the United Biscuit companies together at one headquarters in London. All the family members involved with production, and I who was most intimately involved, came here, so we were no longer really close to production. John Mann had just joined us from Unilever. He became my right-hand man, and he advised us that as we were now operating in a marketing and computer age we were far too production-led and we must change our stance.

It was good advice: we were very, very good at production, but we were not good on marketing. Certainly, in the 1950s I don't think I understood the difference between selling and marketing. But sadly, looking back, we made a complete volte-face, turning all our energies to marketing. Over the next decade production efficiency stood still, allowing our competitors to catch up.

We were still doing well, and we thought that we were so good at production that it would just carry on by itself. But top management was not paying enough attention to it. The further away you are from production, the less likely you are to manage it well.

During this period the factories were being rationalized and reorganized. We closed three in Scotland, concentrating production in one big factory there and several others in England. We were so busy closing factories and reorganizing that we didn't have the resource to ensure that we were installing the best, new technology. This is a very capital-intensive business, and because of the total cost involved we moved old machinery that might have been seven or eight years old, instead of buying state-of-the-art technology.

I wasn't closely enough involved personally, and we had no one else working in the production field with the experience I'd had over sixteen years in creating a really good factory. But we thought we had done a good job because we were measuring productivity as output per head and it was holding up well. We should have been looking instead at unit labour costs – they were rising and that should never have been allowed to happen.

At the same time that all of this was happening we also went into snacks, buying Meredith & Drew in 1967 and Kenyon Son & Craven in 1968. So I was busy broadening the base of the business and concentrating on marketing. Instead, I should have concentrated on production and let John Mann and his people get on with the marketing job – they would have done just as well without me.

We sorted it out eventually, and in recent years our unit labour costs have been steadily decreasing. There's nothing clever about business. I've been in the business my family founded for 45 years and it never occurred to me to do anything else. I've loved it.

All you need to do is have good people, pay them well, invest and buy good machinery – the latest – and you have to advertise, of course. That way you give the consumer good value for money.

But if you forget any one of these, you're in trouble. To make sure you're doing it right, you need to have the right yardsticks with which to measure performance. It's like flying aeroplanes: although there are lots of instruments, you learn to look at the main one which tells you several things. If that is showing the right signals you fly very safely. We should have been looking at unit labour costs; they are vital. It is rising unit labour costs which are one of the major causes of our current economic difficulties.

20 May 1990

Richard Giordano

Richard Giordano was born in New York City in 1934 and studied at Harvard College, going on to read law at Columbia. He left law practice to join Airco Inc. He became CEO in 1978, at 44, and agreed to merge his company with Britain's BOC. When he arrived in 1979 as the group's new CEO, he commanded the highest salary ever paid to a UK industrial director, £271,000. He added the title of BOC chairman in 1985, sits on various company boards and is an honorary KBE.

Back in the middle of the 1960s, when I was 30 years old, I gave up the practice of law and began my business career with Airco, the company I eventually ran as chief executive when BOC took it over in 1978. My first business assignment was marketing vice-president for a division of Airco that distributed and sold industrial gases and welding and cutting equipment to a chain of distributors throughout the United States.

One of our products was helium, which was being used for high-quality welding. Although I didn't have a marketing background, I concluded that there was clearly a market for helium in non-industrial applications, including filling balloons. It wasn't too common then for small balloons to be filled with helium, but little kids loved them. I reckoned there would be a sizeable market, enabling us to increase our sales of helium on a large scale, but the question was how to promote and reach such a market.

I decided that we would get someone to design an attractive clown face and find some way to hook that up with the equipment needed to dispense the helium. We found a designer, and he developed a very pretty plastic, coloured clown's face with a big smile. It was four and a half feet high and two and a half feet wide, big enough to hide the helium tank and delivery equipment, with a dispenser coming out of the clown's mouth. It was a very clever design. The idea was that we'd get lots of these dispensers spread around the country. We said to our 300 distributors that we and you are going to promote helium with 'Windy the Clown'. We're going to lease or sell you these Windys on very favourable terms, and you're going to sell lots of helium. We found suppliers and spent $1m or more buying in thousands of Windys. We thought we'd revolutionize the helium market. Three years later we had an awful lot of Windys that had never left the warehouse, and an awful lot of Windys had been returned.

We thought that because our distributors made a good profit in selling helium, they'd want to increase their sales. Basically, we thought we could get industrial distributors to promote and sell consumer products. With hindsight, had we gone to, say, Sears or other well-known consumer retail chains, we'd probably have succeeded. As it was, we had those Windys sitting in our warehouses for an awfully long time. Eventually we sold them off to those of our industrial distributors, who had a more consumerist turn of mind, and they hired them out to student entrepreneurs who went around funfairs and circuses selling balloons.

Looking back, I don't suppose my boss really knew about it until after it had failed. I had a fair degree of autonomy, and I had told him about it. In fact, I think, even if he had been more aware of it he would have thought it a good idea, though maybe not carried out that way.

But with no marketing training, it was not surprising that I made such a mistake. This all happened in 1966–7, and in 1968 I was promoted. I suspect the real magnitude of the failure only came home to roost after I'd been promoted, but because I'd gone to the next job up, effectively I was my new boss, evaluating my own mistake.

I learned two lessons from this flop. First, industrial and consumer distribution channels are apples and oranges, and you confuse the two at your peril. And second, no matter how fast-track or talented your people may be, there is no substitute for experience. Although a trained lawyer, I knew nothing about marketing and it certainly showed.

It is something I have been aware of in business ever since. If you are moving someone out of functions to line management, it is better for them to make a sideways move – maybe even slightly downwards – to allow them to get that necessary experience.

27 May 1990

Joe Palmer

Joe Palmer CBE, 59, went to King's School, Bruton, Somerset and Trinity College, Cambridge. He joined Legal & General at 24, becoming group chief executive in 1984. He is chairman of the Association of British Insurers and chairs an Industrial Society commmmittee on careers for women in insurance. He is also a member of the President's Committee of Business in the Community, a trustee of the Shakespeare Globe Trust and an honorary fellow of the London Business School.

My biggest mistake was trying to turn a group of non-viable businesses into profit-earners. In 1978 I was made general manager of Legal & General International. This was a new grouping within Legal & General group, which incorporated our life and general insurance businesses in France, Spain and Australia as well as the Victory reinsurance business, both UK and overseas. Until then we had never tried to pull them together under one reporting arrangement. But in all they were losing very large sums of money. It was my job to take responsibility for these businesses, develop a unifying strategy and make them profitable.

We'd been doing business in these countries for a long time. Before World War II we'd started up the Australian general business ourselves, under the Legal & General name. The life business, which we'd begun in the 1950s, was very successful, but general insurance was losing money.

It was the same in France. Here, while we had set up the life business, we inherited the general insurance side when we acquired Gresham in the 1930s. The business in Spain, where both life and general were making a loss, had all been inherited through the Gresham acquisition.

Pre-war it had been almost impossible to lose money on general insurance in mainland Europe. But after the war it became much more competitive. We were told by our managers and agents that to sell life assurance we had also to sell cheap motor insurance as a loss leader to entice intermediaries to take our business. It worked as a ploy but we lost a great deal of money on claims on the motor policies. We were taking big losses for what were tiny companies.

My assessment was that the losses were due to poor management. I thought we could improve the management, reduce expenses and review pricing – all the usual things you do to recover a business. But with the insurance business there really needs to be a sizeable core of overhead. There must be a sufficient level of premium income to support that overhead and to meet the claims. In effect, there is a viability threshold.

It was a matter of painful trial and error that convinced me a viability threshold existed and that it was a relatively high one. I found out the hard way and it took me a long time, about two years, to do so. At that point I told the group we were never going to rise above the threshold and it would be in the shareholders' interests for us to pull out.

We decided to pull out of the general insurance market in Australia and France and out of Spain entirely. At the time it seemed wrong to be pulling out of Europe because one could already discern single market trends. In fact, had we moved a year earlier, we would have saved the Legal & General shareholders a lot of money.

The whole exercise left me with a very strong feeling that where you see the signs of a non-viable business it is in everybody's interests to move quickly and decisively. We didn't recognize fast enough that these businesses were too small to be made viable and for too long the efforts of my colleagues and myself were focused on making them more profitable.

Strategic development isn't just about developing new business. You also need to be very, very objective about existing activities. Of course, you start by thinking you can turn a loss-making business around but pulling out means people lose their jobs which makes it very difficult to say enough's enough, we're closing down.

I think, too, that there is a lot of built-in resistance in any organization to pulling out of a market. It's an admission of failure and there's a certain *amour propre* in staying in that market. Happily, while I learned the lesson, I haven't really needed it since, because we cleared the stables at that stage and weren't left with any marginal businesses.

10 June 1990

Charles Runge

Charles Runge, 46, went to Eton and Christ Church College, Oxford. He joined Tate & Lyle in 1967, and in 1978 was appointed chief executive of Tate & Lyle Refineries to oversee the rationalization of the cane sugar refining industry in the UK. He became managing director of Tate & Lyle's agricultural division in 1983, and then spent two years as director of corporate affairs. He is married with three children, and enjoys music, fishing, walking and computers.

I worked in the sugar industry since leaving university, until I joined the Milk Marketing Board as chief executive in 1988. And my biggest mistake is one I have only recognized in the past twelve months.

My father milked a dozen or so beloved Guernsey cows with names like Annabelle and Verbena. So I knew that the MMB wasn't the fusty-dusty, typewriter-ridden organization of its popular misconception, but it was in actual fact an organization wanting to move ahead and develop its framework of 60 years' standing.

The mistake I made was that I assumed that part of my job would be to convince dairy farmers of the need to move towards an open-market pricing system. As it turned out, the real challenge has been to persuade the board's customers – the manufacturing industry – not the farmers.

Although many individual companies want to move ahead, the majority of them feel much more comfortable in the managed market that currently exists, where milk is allocated to them under a formula based upon their use of it. On the one hand, I found that the dairy producers of England and Wales – some 32,000 of them – were very relaxed with their relationship with their board. The board is a producer-owned co-operative, controlled by the farmers themselves with a chairman elected from among their number.

The present chairman has a very strong belief that farmers should own everything, control everything, but manage nothing. The net effect is that the board's policy is laid down firmly by the dairy producers themselves, and its execution is carried out by a professional cadre of managers. I found myself the leader of that cadre.

Over the years, the MMB has adapted to the environment in which it finds itself. On a macro scale, when quotas were imposed almost overnight in 1984 and milk production was cut back by some 15 per cent, it changed fundamentally from an organization seeking markets for ever-increasing quantities of milk (production was growing at 2 per cent per annum) to an organization managing supply under shortage conditions.

I arrived just as the industry was coming to terms with its changed circumstance. Employment at the MMB has been cut back by around 20 per cent since that time to a shade over 2,600. Yet, the fact is we still collect from 32,000 dairy farms every day, whatever the weather, and deliver to more than 300 dairies. When measured by turnover, the board is the tenth largest food company in Europe, and second only to Nestlé among dairy companies. Yet it is able to move with a speed which would even be a credit to much smaller organizations.

I had assumed when I joined that the rest of the trade was similar, but in practice the dairy industry – though dominated by five or six major companies – consists of many medium-sized and small ones. One of the things the MMB failed to do properly was to look after both its large and small customers – indeed, when I arrived they were called 'buyers' and treated as such.

I have now spoken to nearly all of our customers in one way or another, and it is quite clear that many of them really have to look to their laurels if we, as an industry, are going to compete effectively against the supremely efficient and very large, vertically integrated co-operatives of Europe on the one hand and the growing buying power of the trans-national retailers on the other.

The battle will not be for the purse of 50 million consumers in Island England, but for the purses of 350 million people in Fortress Europe. If I had known how long it would take to change the system of supplying milk in England and Wales, I think I would say that I had made a second major mistake – not having made a major career change ten years earlier!

17 June 1990

Tim Waterstone

Tim Waterstone started his eponymous book retail chain in 1982 after he had been sacked by W H Smith. Born in 1939 he read English at St Catherine's, Cambridge, before becoming a marketing manager at Allied Breweries. He then worked for W H Smith finally becoming chairman of the group's US subsidiary. With Waterstone's he proved that a good bookseller could be successful. In 1989 he struck a deal whereby W H Smith will buy Waterstone's in 1993 for a minimum £40m.

I find it very easy to decide my biggest mistake, and that is that I did not start Waterstone's many years earlier.

As it was, we sold our first book on 1 September 1982 in one small 2,000 square foot store in South Kensington. We had an equity value of £2,000 and seven staff. Today, almost exactly eight years later, with sales nearing £100m, with more than 1,600 staff and more than 400,000 square feet of bookselling space, we are established by far as the largest chain of booksellers in Britain.

The eight years – the most exhilarating of my life – have used up my forties. Exactly the same could have been achieved had I had the courage to have launched the company in 1972 rather than a decade later. The opportunity was always there.

But I was caught in the tender trap of working for a large company. Personal financial obligations were such that the security of corporate life and a regular salary made risking everything on a start-up an unlikely prospect. As every conventional middle-class male knows, mortgages have to be paid, children clothed and educated and the family maintained, and most of our lives become locked into a perpetual cycle of trying to fulfil all the needs of the family.

Then I lost my job. I was working as chairman of W H Smith's US subsidiary when I was fired in 1981. Suddenly I was presented with a choice of how to spend the rest of my life. The plunge into freedom immediately seemed easy, and the total clarity of the sort of company I wanted to put together, and the way Waterstone's should be presented to the public, helped me both to find financial backers comparatively easily and to develop a reputation with the public.

When Waterstone's got under way the average value of stock per square foot across all booksellers was under £40, and sales per square foot were under £140. One fed upon the other; with the trade becoming used to a stock presentation that was simply inadequate to satisfy the public – we reckoned then, and we still do, that a decent general bookseller cannot do a proper job with fewer than 40,000 individual titles in stock at any one time - we told our backers that we would be stocking our shops at at least twice the industry average.

With stock at double the industry average at £80 per sq ft (more than £120 per sq ft now), we felt that sales of £300 per sq ft were easily achievable, and it is at this level that selling books (with controlled occupancy costs) becomes very profitable.

It really is strange that the situation had been allowed to degenerate to the level it had. In France particularly, but certainly in Germany as well, really good stockholding bookshops were trading all over the land ever since the post-war recovery had settled in. But when an industry starts to talk itself into a cycle of defeat the momentum becomes irresistible. The myth of inevitable failure hung over everything the bookselling trade did and said. The perceived wisdom was that only W H Smith, operating very much in the middle and popular area, was viable.

Nobody spent any money, and nobody opened any bookshops of any size. Even Dillons, purchased by Pentos in 1977, remained quiescent and dormant for ten years or so. The French and Germans could make money from bookselling, and the Americans – through B Dalton and Walden, and a number of lively regional chains – could move into a period of vigorous development, but here in Britain failure was the certainty, and the total dominance of the publisher over the retailer accepted as the natural course of affairs.

Venture and development capital for unquoted companies was certainly very much less available in the 1970s than a decade later, but I never cease to bless my luck that nobody else struck for the opportunity when it was there.

                                                                    6 July 1990

Anthony Saxton

Anthony Saxton was born in 1934 in Suffolk. Educated at Harrow he
started medical school, hated it and left to join the Royal Navy. He
began his commercial career at 21 as a London dustman, moving into
marketing at Goya. The experience gained there took him to G-Plan
Furniture where he became international director at 28. In 1964, he
went into advertising and, after working for five agencies, joined an
executive-search consultancy in 1978. In 1986, he set up Saxton
Bampfylde, a successful headhunting agency, with Stephen
Bampfylde.

My biggest mistake was to ignore a great opportunity by following
convention. It happened in 1973 when I was first offered the chance to
become a headhunter and turned it down.

I had been working in advertising for nine years. It was a wonderful
time to be in the ad industry in London: it was the swinging sixties and
London felt like the centre of the world.

I was at an agency called PKL, which had a terrific reputation, when
another, much bigger agency called Vernons poached me. They wanted
me to come in and help turn around the business – which we succeeded
in doing. From Vernons I was headhunted to turn around another agency,
a big US group called NCK. But after two years I fell out with my boss
and was fired. That was 1973, and they gave me a big pay-off, affording
me the chance to think about my career.

An old friend called John Stork (now deputy chairman of Korn/Ferry)
invited me to go into partnership with him to start up an executive search
firm. At the time executive search, or headhunting, was an unusual,
almost exotic method of recruiting very senior people. The industry was
very small, with only a handful of firms, mostly American, in the
business. John proposed to start from scratch, offering me a 40 per cent
stake in the firm. But I was offered another ad agency to turn around – it
was familiar ground so I took the job. It was not so much an active
rejection of head hunting, more that one was brought up to favour
conventional choices in career development.

For the next five years, John kept after me to come and join him. During that time headhunting grew very fast, becoming the normal way of finding board level people for UK companies. I introduced John to many of his early clients and indeed some of his colleagues. Increasingly I became very excited about executive search, seeing the attractions of something that was so involved in change and the future.

In 1978, in my early 40s, I joined John Stork & Partners, though as a well-paid partner with a tiny equity holding instead of a 40 per cent stakeholder. I had also realized that headhunting is a profession where wisdom and experience command a premium.

I became the managing partner of the London office and hired my future partner, Stephen Bampfylde. He built up a successful financial services practice, and he and I left in 1986 to start up Saxton Bampfylde. I was only thirteen years late in getting my own partnership in executive search.

Stephen and I were very fortunate and in just two and a half years we made it into the top ten search firms, then as now dominated by the US-owned international networks. If I had only done it sooner we might have been even more fortunate.

With the benefit of hindsight after twelve years in headhunting, I have noticed that despite conventional career advice, it is becoming more acceptable to make major career changes. In fact it is a sign of someone who can join a business and really change things, that his or her career will have had one or two changes of direction.

I am beginning to notice more and more that with senior jobs clients are beginning to share this perception. It is often smarter to choose people for their ability rather than because they've got experience in a particular industry. So I look out now for people who have had really significant changes of direction in their careers. I just wish I had made my own sooner.

16 September 1990

Sir Gordon Jones

Sir Gordon Jones, 63, was born in Swansea, South Wales, and read chemistry at university. He joined the Navy, moving to the British Iron and Steel Research Association in 1951. He then worked for Esso Petroleum but returned to the steel industry. After several years in Sheffield, he became managing director of Firth Vickers and then a main board director of TW Ward in 1979. In 1983, he was appointed chairman of Yorkshire Water. As chairman of the Water Authorities Association from 1985 to 1989, he led the negotiations on privatization.

In 1968, I became director and general manager of an Essex-based business making ferro-alloys of the sort used extensively by the steel industry. I had just spent several years working as sales and marketing director of a steel alloys maker in Sheffield, which was one of the many merged into British Steel Corp that year. My new firm was a major supplier of ferro-alloys to BSC. Indeed, the group was our biggest customer.

Renationalization at BSC included centralizing many of the group's functions. Only about a month or so after I joined my new company, BSC set up a central purchasing unit headed by a tough, no-nonsense ex-diplomat. In future I would be dealing with it and not my former contacts.

Being new to the ferro-alloy business, I took the view – wrongly as it turned out – that, as the major UK producer, it was down to us to act both as market and price leader. When BSC's purchasers subsequently asked my company for tender prices for ferro-alloys, I quoted what I thought were sensible prices, including a reasonable profit margin.

In doing so, I made two major mistakes. One was in not recognizing that the ferro-alloy market was an international one and there were many other producers just as big as us, or even bigger, on the Continent and elsewhere, which were also bidding for BSC's business. They quoted competitive prices which were in every case lower than the ones I had submitted.

My second mistake was in not recognizing that as a new department, BSC's central purchasing unit would wish to establish its reputation and to show significant cost savings, even if this meant taking tough decisions about some of its suppliers.

I had totally misjudged the situation, and it was hardly surprising that BSC decided to make an example of me and my company by giving us no business that contractual year. As BSC was our largest customer, this was a major blow to me and the company.

After the initial shock wore off, I recognized that I would need to do something very quickly to replace the lost business. Fortunately, through a lot of hard work and overseas travel, my colleagues and I were able to fill the plant with export orders, albeit at lower prices, which had an effect on profits.

But just to compound my problems, I mentioned the story to a local newspaper journalist that I knew in Sheffield. A day or so later, an article appeared saying that BSC had decided to purchase all its ferro-alloys overseas, and I found myself in considerable trouble with my parent company because BSC, justifiably, resented the implications of the article.

Fortunately, in the end, the company took the view that everyone was entitled to make a few mistakes in a new job, even though I had come close to exceeding my quota within the first few weeks, and I survived. While I was with the company, it never really re-established its position with BSC, although it did become a supplier again.

The principal lessons I learned from all this were that one should form an accurate understanding of one's own company's position and strength in the market and also ascertain the motivation – both personal and corporate – of one's major customers, so that a match can be achieved.

In addition, the role of price leader should only be attempted if one's company is truly in that position. It was a painful lesson, but one that I took very much to heart in later business life, and have never forgotten.

30 September 1990

Sir Neville Bowman-Shaw

Sir Neville Bowman-Shaw, 60, is chairman of Lancer Boss. After serving with the Dragoon Guards in the Middle East, he founded the company in 1957 to make and sell front and sidelift trucks. The group is now the largest British-owned lift truck manufacturer, with world-wide sales of more than £175m and a strong reputation for product development. A prominent member of the local Conservative Party, he keeps rare breeds of sheep and cattle and a large collection of vintage tractors at his 2,000-acre farm at Toddington Manor.

I think my biggest mistakes were made in 1972. There were three, but the effects didn't appear until 1974.

We began in 1957 and had a more than acceptable record of growth and new product development, winning three Design Council awards. With a burgeoning market and delivery times going out to twelve months, we needed to increase the volume of production.

The first mistake was doing something because a grant was available, rather than viewing the grant as a bonus. We took a major new factory in Peterlee, which was more than 200 miles from our home in Leighton Buzzard. The second was not fully understanding the effects of high gearing. But the worst was to standardize on key proprietary components and to source them from a single supplier without confirmation that they could and would perform.

The crisis peaked in July 1974, when against a scheduled requirement of several hundred engines of one type we received fewer than 50. It was terrible and we became progressively highly geared and unstable. We were in real trouble. It led to us having three overlapping waves of redundancies. The payroll fell by just over half.

The first breakthrough came when Ford said they would deliver an additional 200 engines a month. They kept pouring these engines into us as agreed, which – thank God – enabled us to survive. The other was a consequence of having a machine copied by a competitor. We took out a patent action and won nearly £600,000 damages in December 1974, which was a great boost to confidence. Everybody thought I was being obsessive about it, but I believed we were right. It was about the third biggest settlement in engineering in those days.

Between 1972 and 1975 we hovered between profit and loss before strong recovery from 1976. One of the results of the large-scale redundancies was that whole departments had to go. I agreed to eliminate new product development and it led to us losing our technical product leadership in the late 1970s and I don't think we really got it back until 1983.

Today, we have recovered product leadership and claim one of the most comprehensive and modern lift truck ranges in the world. In addition, we design, manufacture and supply electric and diesel lift trucks and electric very narrow aisle trucks to such companies as Komatsu and Nissan of Japan and Clark of America. We acquired Germany's third largest lift truck manufacturer in 1983 and the leading Spanish manufacturer in 1985. Through these wholly-owned subsidiaries, we have substantial design and manufacturing operations in three of the five major European Community economies.

Looking to the future, I would say that we are fortunate in being a private company. I am very keen on new product development, but evolving a new product range is a long haul. To get a fully up-to-date product range can take ten years, and that is with a highly skilled and experienced group. By contrast, developing a strong management team will take one year and will be refined within three. And when you compare this with funding, which might take six to twelve months, you can understand my obsession with product in the development of the company and its recovery. Being a private company, Lancer Boss Group can continue a high level of new product investment, without pressures from external shareholders.

7 October 1990

David Woods

David Woods, 42, was born in Liverpool and took masters degrees at both Cambridge and Sheffield University. He joined Equity & Law Life Assurance in 1969 and in 1979 went to Equity & Law's Netherlands operation where he was assistant manager for four years. In 1986, he joined Royal Life before moving to Scottish Provident in 1988 and becoming managing director that July. He is a non-executive director of Lautro, and a fellow of the Institute of Actuaries and the Royal Statistical Society.

Even though I knew that changing a company's culture takes four or five years, I made the mistake of losing patience with my company and trying to rush it.

It happened at Scottish Provident where I have been managing director since July 1988. When I joined, the company had really solid foundations and a good track record for our policy holders, built up by my predecessor. The company was poised to go into the 1990s with good employees, assets and brandname. But Scottish Provident was a fairly typical mutual life assurance company, rather conservative in its business, although people in the company were ready for change and were enthusiastic about it.

I started by restructuring the senior management team and formalizing the planning structure. By the end of my first six months I was ready to stand up at our annual conference and give them an 'up and at 'em' speech. I wanted to open minds and raise ambitions so that I could focus on changing the culture. I was not too specific about the detail at that point.

Over the following year we created a structure for new product development and pushed cultural change further down the organization. It was hard for people, and learning to do things a new way often means you do not at first do them as well as the old way. It takes time to adjust and become efficient. I should have ensured that people not only understood what we were trying to do but also had a means of telling us that at times we were going too fast, but I did not.

By the end of 1989 I thought that the organization was ready to concentrate on new product development, a key area. Before I came the group had been developing less than one major product a year. During 1989 we managed two substantial new products and at the year-end conference I stood up and set targets for three very specific new products to come out during the first half of this year, and a commitment to start developing another two or three.

In the end, the first product took more resources and effort than we thought it would, the second had to be jettisoned and the third, an important new range of pension products, was three months late. Of the other three products in development, one might make it this year, another has been abandoned and the third will definitely not come to market until next year. This happened because I had seriously underestimated the time and effort involved in working this culture change.

I think I got the big picture right but I failed to recognize that to get from A to B, we might need to go via C or even D. Had I listened, my people could probably have told me that. You have got to make a culture change very participative if you are to take people along with you. The planning cycle for 1991, already under way, involves more people. We are getting opinions on the art of the possible from lower down in management and we have a much clearer view of strategy.

So my mistake was to be impatient. When I sat down at the beginning I thought to myself that this process will take four or five years. But when I started to put it into practice I was perhaps arrogant in thinking I could push it through more quickly. Now I know I cannot.

The lesson has been two-way. I have learned to be more patient and the organization has gone through a bit of a shock. If a shock's not too severe it can shorten the process of change by giving it a bit of a kick. So now I hope it will take us only four years.

28 October 1990

Sophie Mirman

Sophie Mirman, 34, rose from the typing pool at Marks & Spencer to be managing director of Tie Rack. With her husband, Richard Ross, she started up Sock Shop in 1983, going public in 1987. She was voted both USM Entrepreneur and Businesswoman of Year in 1988. But a rapid expansion into the United States brought trouble and the shares were suspended in February 1990. Administrators sold the business in August. The couple then opened a shop called Trotters.

My biggest mistake was definitely taking Sock Shop to America. It was a disaster. After we floated the company in 1987, we were approached by an experienced retailer who lived in America and felt sure that Sock Shop would work there.

We had 50 shops here at the time, and we had thought about moving overseas, but not for quite a while. Maybe in two or three years' time, and certainly not to the States. Much more likely we would have expanded to France, since I'm of French extraction. But, rather foolishly, we were tempted. America is a huge market, and there is no apparent language barrier. It was only subsequently that we found out just how different it is.

We also thought that we could position the shops in high-pedestrian-flow areas in New York by the subways, just as we had in London. We hadn't appreciated the violence and the number of drug-related attacks that go on in Manhattan. Junkies would just walk in and attack the staff, or hold them at gunpoint, to steal from the till. We used to empty the tills very regularly, but they would still come in just to steal a few dollars. We had to have armed security guards. One shop we moved into had been a candy store. We couldn't understand why junkies kept coming in for the first couple of weeks, until we realized that it had been a front for a drug dealing operation.

Before we started we went to New York and walked the streets. We saw the department stores and the women, who wear tights all year round even if it's 100F outside, and you couldn't tell that America was at the top of its retail boom. We took on an American team, including a hosiery buyer who had previously worked for Saks and knew the US and UK markets. Essentially, we relied on people who knew New York, and they thought we would be perfect.

Here, the City was thrilled when we announced we were going to America. We were being hailed as retail experts then (now we really are). But America is the UK retailer's graveyard. I can't think of a single British retailer who has been able to make America work. The market looks so tempting, but my goodness it taught us a lesson – it cost us the business. If America had been the only problem, I think we could have survived it. But between 1987 and 1989 interest rates doubled and we were highly geared. We'd had a succession of mild winters and hot summers – and sales were right down.

Then there were the transport strikes in 1989: a train and tube strike once a week for fifteen weeks, which meant that a third of our shops, those by stations, were closed one day a week and passenger flow was depressed all summer. So we had three major problems, all outside our control. Meanwhile we were trying to get the stock computerized and put in an electronic point-of-sale system. We just ended up facing all these problems like a rabbit frozen in car headlights. There wasn't anything we could do about it, and the banks couldn't see any way to get their money back except through administration.

Now we have Trotters; the shop sells children's clothing, footwear and accessories. It has a high service element and so isn't the kind of shop you could build into a large chain, so we'll stick to four to six shops at most. I know I said that about Sock Shop, but this time I mean it. And to any other retailer I would say: 'Don't go to America.'

4 November 1990

Norman Willis

Norman Willis, 57, is a life-long trade unionist. Both his parents were shop stewards, and he left grammar school at sixteen to work at the London headquarters of the Transport and General Workers' Union. After national service from 1951 to 1953, he won a TUC scholarship to Ruskin College, Oxford. He then studied philosophy, politics and economics at Oriel College, where he is now an honorary fellow. He returned to the TGWU in 1959, moved to the Trades Union Congress in 1974 and became general secretary ten years later.

My biggest mistake is that I did not take an initiative on women's representation in the structure of the trade union movement earlier. There are several explanations – never excuses, of course – for this. In the six years since I became general secretary there have been the miners strike and the Wapping dispute and a lot of time has been spent trying to sort out divisions within the movement.

And there have been a few achievements. Among these are tackling the nuclear energy issue that threatened to split the organization, the establishment of a special review body that led to a whole series of reforms and new services, setting up a 'union law scheme' covering millions of trade union members that provides free legal advice on any matter excluding employment matters, launching the TUC's own credit card and a recruitment campaign whereby unions compete on excellence but not with each other. But I wish now that we had moved earlier on the role of women within the movement. When Ada Maddocks, this year's president of the TUC, came on the general council in 1977 she was one of two women members. Today there are fifteen.

Much of that is down to a specific initiative that we took last year. I suspect that we are at, or very near, the top of the league of public organizations in that more than a quarter of our governing body are women. And more and more unions have been addressing the issue through special efforts and structures designed to give women a few more of the opportunities that they are entitled to. (As Neil Kinnock would say, 'That's not a favour, that's a right; that's not a favour, that's justice.') At our congresses and at union conferences women are much more part of the scene than previously. Discussions on equality issues are carried out with total seriousness and perhaps without the distinction that you could still see a few years ago. There are more women representatives and there are more women negotiators. But we still have a long way to go.

Unless women workers see the trade union movement as being not only responsive to the needs of women but increasingly run by women, we will not have done what is right and what is necessary. Despite a substantial decline in total membership, the number of women members has increased each year over the last decade. But all this should be seen as an encouragement and not an excuse for complacency.

The plain fact is that within the next five years or so women will make up over half the labour force. There must be a prime opportunity for trade union recruitment. This is not just because of their numbers but also because of their needs.

They will still face inadequacies in training, far below those of their male colleagues, since they will still be expected to do a lowly-paid job while also carrying the bulk of the responsibility for running a home. It does not surprise me that facilities for child care come so high on the agenda for women workers and this issue has to be put higher and higher on the agenda of negotiations.

But if the mistake is qualified by the significant things already achieved, the real lesson is that the best is surely yet to come: many more women delegates at Congress, meetings that are organized at the best times for women to take part and union structures that enable women to come to the fore despite the calls on their time that prevent them spending so much time on union matters.

9 September 1990

John Banham

John Banham is director-general of the Confederation of British Industry. Born in Torquay in 1940, he took a first in Natural Sciences at Queens' College, Cambridge. After five years in industry, in marketing, he joined McKinsey & Co as a management consultant. Gaining industrial experience in the UK, US and Europe, he became, at 40, the youngest-ever British director of McKinsey. In 1983 he became chief executive of the Audit Commission before joining the CBI in 1987.

My biggest mistake was to implement a poor solution to a problem. It happened in 1972, when I was the most junior member of a team of management consultants from McKinsey & Co, sent in by Sir Keith Joseph to reorganize the Department of Health.

We were working for a steering group chaired by the late Sir Philip Rogers, who was then permanent secretary to the Department of Health. This group comprised all the warring factions within the National Health Service. Our job was to come up with the proposals to bring the hospitals, community care and family practitioners (GPs, dentists and pharmacists) together in one integrated service and for the management structure required to run it. But during our work, two of us realized that the terms of reference we had been given were fundamentally wrong in the first place. The white paper we were implementing set out that the boundaries of the health authorities were to be exactly the same as those for the social services – in other words based on county borders.

This was a fundamental error: health care is a local thing, and the flow of patients to a hospital does not necessarily follow county boundaries. Neither do county boundaries necessarily make regions of a suitable size for management purposes. That meant that we needed to set up sub areas and even districts, making management very complicated.

My mistake was in realizing that what we were being asked to do did not make sense but failing to push my concerns and convictions as hard as I could have done. We drew it to the attention of our partner at McKinsey, and he advised us to tell it to Sir Philip. But he said it had all been agreed by Cabinet and was not going to be changed now. Our job was to get on and make the new arrangements work. At that point,

McKinsey said our duty was to serve the interests of the client (although there is always a question of who the client is when it comes to public service!).

I have reproached myself for what happened ever since. We could have pushed our partner to get him to withdraw McKinsey from the job. We might have averted what turned out to be unnecessary mistakes which had to be undone later in subsequent reorganizations. But what was put in place was expensive and entailed adding bureaucracy. And, arguably, the NHS lost at least five years of management improvement because of it.

I subsequently published a report saying in effect that the service needed to be integrated at the district level, with money flowing direct from Parliament. Instead of having all that hierarchy in between, it simply needed an independent National Health Service Board. This is now what the Government is doing with the NHS.

I learned some very important lessons from this. The first is that, you should never go along with something that you do not believe is right, however much the experts say it is. The second is that solutions to complex problems with which all the interested parties agree, are probably not solutions at all. The third is that, in this situation, it is better to put what you believe to be the right solutions on the table and let them be shot at, rather than to try the lowest common denominator solutions.

I have spent the rest of my career determined not to go along with whatever happens to be today's received wisdom, but to try to do what I think is right.

11 November 1990

Chris Lane

Chris Lane is the chief executive and major shareholder of the time management training company TMI UK. Born in Cornwall in 1943, he attended Oxford University, before spending fifteen years with an international service company. He set up TMI UK in 1978, and was personally involved in the introduction of the Putting People First programme to British Airways, which ultimately led to TMI running the programme for 40,000 staff over eighteen months. He still presents TMI programmes all over the world.

My mistake was expecting Americans to adopt a European idea too quickly. The situation arose when we took over control of the two US companies that had been set up by the Danish group TMI A/S.

TMI in Denmark had set up a San Francisco company in 1980 and a New York business in 1984 to sell its training programmes in time management and other personal productivity skills. Europeans were put in to run the businesses instead of using local managers. Neither company talked to the other, and they were not doing all that well.

In 1986, TMI Denmark handed over the companies to us – TMI (UK) – at a time when we were doing very well in the UK with our courses in corporate culture change. We had started these in the early 1980s with the Putting People First programme for British Airways. This side of the business expanded rapidly.

We wanted to introduce this programme in the US to go along with the skills training we already did there. The American market looked promising because we had already worked for American Express in the UK and Europe and they had asked us to run a course for them in the US. We did this very successfully using our US consultants. I also wanted to replace the European managers in the US with qualified Americans. We found an American president and based him at the New York office, and began integrating the companies, including the sub-agencies we had set up.

We brought the American president here to be interviewed and he subsequently came over on several week-long visits. We thought we had given him enough to absorb the TMI vision, but we underestimated the amount of time and face-to-face communication needed to do so.

The training market in the US, which is pretty well developed, is also rather conservative in its approach. It calls for traditional techniques of skills training rather than an all-embracing challenge to culture and values, which is what our programmes are all about. So the president and his management team were always trying to dress up the programmes as 'skills training'. This only succeeded in blurring the course concept, rather than selling its uniqueness to the market.

The other problem was that our president, who was a brilliant, conceptual developer, spent two years reinventing the product rather than selling it. The truth is the product needed upgrading and he contributed some good ideas but we lost valuable time and considerable cash in the process.

We gave the Americans too much rope, too much freedom, and not enough time, money or understanding of the product to do the job well. We failed to understand how different the market there was, or even that the regional markets there can be very different. It cost us two and a half years and $2.5m.

The president left in April, and we appointed one of his managers to the job. Now we sell the programme on its own merits, by keeping the message simple. We try to get across the idea that if you want to improve customer service it's easy to teach new skills. But a quantum leap only comes from changing attitudes right through the organization. We're doing much better, even in today's tougher market, and have closed a deal with four major customers, two of which are now up and running. Having made losses in the US in 1989 and 1990, we should make a profit in 1991.

18 November 1990

Sir Peter Walters

Sir Peter Walters was appointed chairman of British Petroleum in November 1981 and retired this March. Born in Birmingham in 1931, he went to King Edward's School and Birmingham University. After military service he joined BP in 1954, working in international oil supply and development and regional management. He was appointed managing director in 1973. He is currently a non-executive director of SmithKline Beecham, deputy chairman of Thorn EMI and chairman of Blue Circle.

My mistake was to believe that diversification was BP's solution to the oil crisis of the 1970s.

In 1973 I was managing director of BP when we suffered the first of the oil crises. During that time many of the oil-producing countries nationalized Western companies which extracted oil there.

At home many of the consumer countries had socialist or corporatist governments which wanted to regulate the industry. The Wilson government formed British National Oil Corporation, BNOC, and even the US was talking about a federal oil and gas company. In the resultant squeeze, the oil companies began to lose confidence. They started to question their future roles. I, along with the other directors of BP, took the view that we should diversify.

Over the next few years we moved into coal, minerals and information technology (as well as nutrition, which was a successful move). Like others in the industry, we felt we could adduce synergy from these businesses because they seemed like natural extensions of what we already did. But what we found was that in coal we did not have the resource base and market share, and there was not much opportunity in the industry to differentiate the product from anyone else's. In minerals we lacked knowledgeable exploration activity, and in IT we were experienced users, not providers.

I became chairman of BP in 1981 and the following year we lost £600m in our European oil, chemicals and shipping businesses. We also had extensive duplication of our operations in the US because of part ownership of Standard Oil.

I set BP to looking at all its businesses with two vital criteria in mind–critical mass and selective excellence. These can be applied to any business. For the first, you should ask whether the business has a big enough market share to compete effectively and generate a strong cash flow. If so, does it offer customers the second? This will be appropriate to the business, research and development in specialty chemicals, for example, new products in electronics or a thorough understanding of the customer base in the rentals business.

If a business possesses both qualities then it should aim to be one of the top three businesses that people think of in its field. If it is not then you should think about either getting to that position or else leaving the business. With BP, it was often a question of either doubling the size of the businesses or getting out.

Over the next four years we dramatically rationalized our operations in Europe and the US. Next we got out of coal and sold our IT business, Scicon, and our minerals business to RTZ. The pity was that if, in the first place, we had put even half of the effort we put into diversifying into our core business it would have paid off. But the grass was greener.

The lesson on diversification has been borne out by companies such as BP, which got out and survived and prospered, along with those which remained over-diversified and failed – the Alan Bonds and John Gunns of this world. I now believe that directors' responsibilities to shareholders require them to be much more aware of the potential waste of diversifying.

Real conglomerates such as Hanson and BTR have no particular attachment to any one business and run them all very objectively. But an oil man will try to look for a synergy in minerals or coal that does not really exist.

9 December 1990

Tom Farmer

Tom Farmer, 50, grew up in Leith, Edinburgh and left school at fifteen to work for a local tyre firm. At 20 he was a salesman for Goodyear. At 24 he started his own tyre business which he sold at 28, subsequently retiring to the US. But at 31 he came back to the UK to start an exhaust business called Kwik-Fit which now has a turnover of £193m. He has been commended by Parliament and pressure groups alike for his contributions to the safety of children on British roads.

Expanding too rapidly through acquisition was probably the biggest business mistake I ever made. I had started Kwik-Fit in 1971 and we built the company up to 49 depots, all north of Manchester, by 1980.

We had a clear corporate identity with our blue and white logo and blue overalls, an excellent reputation with customers, and a good financial control system. By the late-1970s we were thinking of expansion. Towards the end of 1979 we approached a competitor, Euro Exhausts, which had 51 depots south of Birmingham. We acquired the business in January 1980 for £10m, immediately doubling our size.

Now we felt we were really king of the castle, with a national business. We were also excited because our suppliers kept telling us about Euro's computer system and we thought we could just slide our way of controlling the business into their system. The biggest shock came when we discovered that their computer system just produced reams of paper and required even more administrative staff than we had.

We also wanted to change the company's name to Kwik-Fit Euro and create a single company identity. But they had a yellow and brown logo and brown overalls and this turned out to be a very contentious issue. Whose colours would win? And we wanted the managers of Euro to do things our way. They didn't want to, so they left the company.

Three months later we were still struggling to put the thing together, desperately short of management, when another deal came along. I made inquiries and found that the Firestone Tyre company had 180 retail depots but was thinking of selling them to concentrate on manufacturing. A month later I met the managing director in London and we did the deal that day. I had to – at £3.25m it was a snip.

Flying back to Edinburgh I knew it would be a bit of a problem breaking the news. So I told the other managers we were a national company and had to keep on expanding. I'm a wee bit of an orator, and as I kept talking they were getting more and more excited. Then I dropped the bombshell and there was a stony silence. Then the boys started flipping their lids.

In the end we did a deal with Dunlop Rubber, which paid £3.25m for 82 of the depots. So in effect we got 98 depots free.

On reflection it was foolhardy to have attempted the Firestone deal. It was a good deal in the end but we were very lucky because I went in without proper planning. Our acquisition turned out to have no financial controls and terrible staff morale. Even worse, the Firestone mechanics wore red overalls, and their signs were all red and white!

Prior to that deal we had produced profits of £4m. Now our turnover had gone up fourfold but our profits fell to £1m. I had to stand up and tell the shareholders that this was due to our investment in the future and all the other things you say at such times.

The whole thing caused us a lot of pain and grief at the time. It took two years of dedication and commitment to integrate the administration and financial controls, bring in a proper computer system and train staff. What I learned is that you should never do anything just because it's a good idea. You must spend time on making sure it's a really good idea. Of course you can add instinct based on experience. But don't go on gut feeling – that's just a recipe for indigestion.

20 January 1991

Nigel Swabey

Nigel Swabey, 42, is chairman of NSP Group, the direct marketing group he founded in 1980. A graduate in business studies and marketing, he spent his early career marketing branded goods. It was his idea to send out mail order catalogues with credit card statements and Sunday supplement magazines. He has scoured the world looking for innovative merchandise, which NSP sells through mail order catalogues such as Quorum, Innovations and The Leading Edge. NSP has a turnover of about £45m.

My biggest mistake was one I made in 1974, when I was 26. I was employed by the merchandise division of Book Club Associates as marketing manager, and we had just launched a mail order business which I later called Kaleidoscope.

A consultant's report had recommended that we should offer furniture to our book club members. We dutifully went to an exhibition at Earls Court and saw some black ash veneer hi-fi cabinets, bookcases and drinks trolleys exhibited by a Dutch company. I was very taken with the stuff and ordered more than £250,000-worth of stock.

Three months later the furniture arrived at our warehouse in Swindon, fully assembled and packed in cartons.

Meanwhile, I had spent £15,000 producing a leaflet called Black Ash, White Light and Greenery. There were seductive shots of the furniture, with a modern white table lamp, surrounded by plants.

The leaflets were inserted with the statements of several hundred thousand book club members. The offer proved very popular and the goods started going out.

A week later they started coming back. I got a call from the warehouse manager to say three hi-fi cabinets and two trolleys had been returned. He said they could not be refurbished and he thought I ought to go and have a look.

When I did finally visit the warehouse, stacked to the ceiling in one corner was the furniture, in various states of disassembly. In fact it was ruined. I had forgotten, when I wrote the order at Earls Court, that for efficient postal delivery, furniture really needs to be packed flat. (If assembled, it should be very well protected.)

My first reaction was to see how much could be saved for possible resale, so I started sorting through the wreckage, separating splintered panels from good ones, putting hinges to one side and so on. I spent two days doing it on my own. I was too ashamed to ask anyone to help me. The experience imprinted itself on my memory and taught me a crucial lesson.

If you are going to despatch ready-assembled goods in a cardboard carton, first drop the carton from a great height, then jump up and down on it and generally smash it about. In other words, give it the sort of treatment the delivery service might.

We had sent the goods out, at vast cost, some with the Post Office and others with a freight company. Everything was marked 'fragile', but that just seemed to encourage our carriers to be even rougher with the goods. Sometimes we had to send four replacements before one would arrive in an undamaged state.

My final agony was the auction. I had only managed to salvage about ten pieces of furniture. People would look at it, kick it and offer a derisory amount. To my shame, I can remember standing at the back of the auction, raising my hand to try and raise the bids.

It was an expensive episode. We had to write off stock worth £50,000 and another £25,000 in lost profit, plus an untold fortune in customer dissatisfaction. In addition, there was the cost of administration, the loss of time, the extra carriage on redelivery and the cost of the auctioneer. It was an important lesson for a career in direct marketing, and fortunately it came early on. Whenever I think of trying to cut corners on packaging I remember it, and have never made a similar mistake since.

27 January 1991

Robert Klapp

Robert Klapp is chairman of Select Appointments, an international recruiting agency which he has built up over the last eight years. Before starting his own business, Mr Klapp was managing director of Reliance, an agency bought by Blue Arrow for £9.9m two years after he left. He worked for Reliance for twelve years. Select, which started with one office in Crawley in 1983, went public in 1987 and now has 55 offices around the world.

My biggest mistake was not having the courage to go out on my own earlier than I did. In 1971, I was working as a branch manager for the recruitment agency Reliance. Together with a colleague, I had made up my mind to start a business. We had found an area that didn't coincide with Reliance's existing business, and a potential office.

But Reliance beat us to it. They too had decided to go into this area, and by coincidence took up the very same unit that we wanted for our office Being relatively inexperienced, we backed off fast. After that I decided to stay on with Reliance. I had a rapid rise in the company and within five years was the managing director. The more I advanced, the less reason there was to leave.

But the stress of working for somebody else finally gave me a heart attack in 1979. My blood pressure was way over the top, and all because I didn't realize how unhappy I was. I never actually achieved the state of mind where I could look at myself and say: 'I know I'm good.' I lacked the confidence. When you are controlling people you never give them that accolade. I was being manipulated all the time. But one day I realized that I really was quite good.

My wife Marianna had opened her own agency in Crawley, Sussex, in the middle of the last recession. By 1982, she was earning money faster than I could spend it. She opened another office in Milton Keynes. Within three months she was making profits there too.

By this time I had been with Reliance for twelve years, but I still didn't own a single share in it. I went to talk to the people I worked for, but they wouldn't let me have any sort of share option. So I suggested they back me in building up a similar business in the provinces. After three or four years, the two could be put together and floated on the stock market. They said no.

I handed in my notice on 1 October 1983 and said I was going to open my own agency. I was told to go straight to my office and not speak to anyone. In twelve years the company had never made a loss, not even in the recession. I had been producing all these profits, yet on my last day the chairman did not even say goodbye.

I went straight to the Business Expansion Scheme and got the backing for Select Appointments, using Marianna's two branches as the foundation for the company. I never realized how much stress I had been under until I made the break. It was as though a massive load had disappeared.

One of the first differences is that you treat your own people a damn sight better. You talk about our company, not my company. I wanted people to be a part of Select, to have shares in it and to be well paid. There is a lady here today who earned £120,000 a couple of years ago. The point is, in the company where I was MD, I would never have been allowed to put in a creative scheme that would generate so much profit for the individuals. Here, if you're successful you get recognition. We love seeing people getting large salary cheques because that tells us that the company's doing well. Everyone in the company is on profit share, including me.

Being too scared to make the move earlier cost me twelve years of my life and up to £30m in lost profits. So my advice to anyone who has got the drive, is just get out and do it. Failing is not about going down, it's about not getting back up again.

3 February 1991

Andrew Gifford

Andrew Gifford, 38, is a lobbyist despite an ill-starred beginning to his career. After reading economics and law at Edinburgh he worked as David Steel's personal assistant for five years. At 28 he set up GJW Government Relations, a lobbying firm which was sold to Lowe Group, part of Interpublic, in 1987 for £6.5m. As GJW's chief executive he specializes in lobbying on behalf of companies. He also shares ownership with Guardian Newspapers of a publishing company called Fourth Estate.

My biggest mistake was one I made early on in my career and concerned the value of discretion. Fresh out of university, I was working as personal assistant to David Steel.

We were in the middle of a leadership campaign between David Steel and John Pardoe. Our campaign was showing Mr Steel as the clean and polished Scotsman, the upright man of the kirk.

At the beginning of the campaign, Cyril Smith had written to David Steel saying that he was not proposing to take sides. But within a matter of weeks he had joined the Pardoe camp so Cyril's letter promising impartiality was shown to the press. Of course he was absolutely furious, and wrote an indignant riposte to Mr Steel.

Days later we all gathered for a by-election. Following one of our constituency meetings I became separated from David Steel in the rush and I hitched a lift to the next meeting with a brace of welcoming hacks. One was a lobby correspondent, the other, from the *Observer*, was not.

During the 20-minute drive, they asked me how the leadership campaign was going. I said, absolutely fine, but feelings are beginning to run in a more lively fashion. What do you mean? they asked.

Well, I said grandly, Cyril's seething at the moment and behaving impossibly. For example, we've just had some extremely silly correspondence, and as an afterthought, I added that he couldn't even spell. (This referred to a spelling mistake in the most recent letter and coming from me – one of the world's worst spellers – was intended merely as a throwaway remark.)

That weekend I went up to Ettrickbridge to stay with the Steels, and on Sunday morning I got up early to fetch all the Sunday papers. Flicking through I was horrified to discover, on page three of the *Observer*, a big piece about the leadership campaign with a banner headline along the lines of 'Liberals in new row' followed by 'Cyril can't even spell, says Steel aide'.

Of course David saw it, and he was not at all amused. He icily explained that this might not be very helpful to the style of his campaign. Fortunately his wife Judy took a lighter view which helped. Rumours came back of Cyril's sensitive feelings on the matter, and I tried hard to avoid him. Eventually Mr Steel won the campaign by a wide margin. A few weeks later, at the first parliamentary meeting I had my dreaded encounter with Cyril Smith. When he saw me he pointed and asked, 'What's he doing here?' David soothed him and the meeting continued, but it took a number of years, if ever, for Cyril to forgive me.

That was one consequence. Another was that the finger was always pointed at me over any dirty tricks or leaks that had occurred during, and after, the leadership campaign. I learnt very quickly what lobby terms (especially concerning journalists and non-attributable quotes) were, and I also learnt very quickly both the benefits and consequences of using the press. That whole leadership campaign was an early lesson for me in campaign and lobbying techniques.

10 March 1991

Greg Stanley

Greg Stanley, 45, could have been running the UK's largest quoted do-it-yourself retail chain by now if he had followed his retailer's instincts in the early 1980s. He grew up in Kent and joined the family business, A G Stanley, at sixteen. He and his brother built up the business which they floated in 1972 and sold in 1988 for £130m. He is now building another DIY business, Focus, which made a profit of £1.9m last year. He is also president and a major shareholder of Brighton and Hove Albion Football Club.

My biggest mistake was sticking to the high street with our do-it-yourself chain, Fads, instead of moving out of town.

My father started A G Stanley, which owned Fads, after the war. As a child I lived over the first shop and I started working in the business when I left school at sixteen. By then we had ten shops in south-east London. My father retired the next year so my brother Malcolm and I ran the business. During the 1960s, Fads expanded until we had about 60 shops. We took on a finance director in 1968 and by 1972 we were able to float the business with a turnover of £3m.

Throughout the 1970s we took over groups of regional shops so that by 1979 we had doubled the size of the chain. Then in 1979 Berger, the paints company, sold us its retail chain of 100 shops for shares, and the chairman of Berger, who was a manufacturer by trade, joined the board as a non-executive director.

Shortly after that we bought another 100 stores from Morris Blakey. Within six months we had just about tripled the size of the company. By the start of the 1980s we were the leading retailer in DIY, with about 350 high street stores.

Early in the 1980s I concluded that we needed to start opening stores out of town. On my travels I had seen retailers in the US moving out of the high streets to big, out-of-town stores. Several grocery and DIY chains were copying them over here.

But I could not persuade the board. Led by my brother, the board felt the business was good the way it was and it was very nervous of changing a successful formula.

Instead they wanted to spend our money on more high street shops – which is what we did. Only Peter Woods and I argued for out-of-town sites. It was very frustrating. We had to turn down Payless, which could have formed the rump of an out-of-town chain.

Other out-of-town chains came up for grabs and went. Alan Foster, who had the leader, B & Q, was a great friend of mine and he used to ask me why we didn't come after his group.

The trouble was, we didn't have enough retailers on the board, and my brother was opposed to out-of-town sites. If we had brought more retailers on to the board this story might have been very different. We had the opportunity to buy 120 superstores in all, which would have put us in the top three DIY chains with a mix of out-of-town and high street shops. In the end, Ward White, which owned the Payless out-of-town chain, offered a good price for A G Stanley in 1988 and we sold the business for £130m. Then Ward White was bought by Boots, which has since merged Payless with W H Smith's Do-It-All.

Since the sale of A G Stanley I have bought two DIY businesses in the North and built a chain of out-of-town stores. We're making good profits but I'd like to add a chain of high street shops. The point is that we didn't have to choose between high street or out-of-town. That was our mistake, we should have done both.

17 March 1991

Lord Marsh

Richard Marsh, 63, has had plenty of opportunities to make mistakes: during his extensive career he has been a trade unionist, a civil servant, Minister of Energy and of Transport, run British Rail and is currently a director or chairman of a number of companies around the world. But he says he really came a cropper in television, when he was deputy chairman and a founder of TV-am. He has most recently been appointed as special UK adviser to Nissan Motor Company, a job he held before for seven years when he helped Nissan establish car plants in Sunderland, Tyne & Wear.

My biggest mistake was falling for an old business chestnut when I was deputy chairman of TV-am, of which I was a founding shareholder along with David Frost and Michael Rosenberg.

When we started the business in 1980, I accepted one of the commonest clichés in the business world, usually expressed when you move to some new type of activity: 'One of the things you'll discover is that this business is quite different and quite special. It isn't like making baked beans.' In this case, from the very beginning, the assumption was that the new breakfast television franchise should be primarily driven by the creative people – presenters and producers – rather than by professional managers. We put together a team known as the Famous Five: Anna Ford, Esther Rantzen, Angela Rippon, Michael Parkinson and Robert Kee. Of course we also had David Frost, who, in addition to having an international reputation as an interviewer, is also an astute businessman.

We won the franchise in 1980 and started broadcasting in 1982, but the thing was an almost unmitigated disaster. The audience just didn't materialize, despite this unique galaxy of talent. Consequently advertisers weren't interested in buying advertising, and the money didn't come in as we had predicted.

Our finances went rapidly out of control. At one stage the revenues were around £300,000 a month while our expenses were running at about £2m and there were bailiffs in the building. Part of the problem was that there was no clear management structure and no clear lines of accountability, but there were, as a result, an awful lot of arguments between the key players.

From the start it was all very extravagant. Our first offices were just off Park Lane. We had studios designed by Terry Farrell and equipped with state-of-the-art equipment. We employed too many people – all because we had absolutely no doubts that as soon as we started broadcasting the audiences would come.

Very belatedly, a group of us on the board took a deep breath and with the threat of an extraordinary general meeting, which would have brought the whole house down, made fundamental changes. It wasn't an enjoyable experience but it enabled us to attract new investment, giving us the opportunity to make a fresh start.

Lord Matthews, then chairman of Fleet Holdings, owners of Express Newspapers, and Kerry Packer, the Australian media tycoon, joined as major investors and also introduced Bruce Gyngell to the board. A widely experienced TV executive, he is rightly credited with much of TV-am's subsequent success. Jonathan Aitken, already an investor through his company Aitken Hume, became chief executive, while I took over the temporary chairmanship for the first stage of the reorganization.

After its shambolic start, TV-am is today accepted as a first-class company, producing first-class television with sophisticated financial controls and some of the tightest manning levels in the industry. In short, it's being managed like any other good business.

Of course, every business needs people who can design the right product, but even with a good product, without tight financial controls and clear lines of accountability from the board down, any business will eventually fail. Never again will I accept that 'this business is quite different from any other'.

24 March 1991

Sir Cyril Smith

Sir Cyril Smith, the prominent Liberal MP, was born in Rochdale in 1928. Poverty and unemployment left their mark and he was determined to have his own business. Leaving school at sixteen he worked as a clerk for the Inland Revenue and began a lifelong involvement with politics. His first business was the newsagents where he had worked as a boy. He sold this and went to work for spring-maker F S Ratcliffe and Sons. In 1963 he started his own, successful spring manufacturing firm and ran it for many years. He rose to become Mayor of Rochdale and chief whip of the Liberal Party.

Outside Rochdale, of course, most folk regard me as a politician. But inside Rochdale they know me as a businessman, too, having run a successful spring manufacturing business for many years.

My spring-making career began when I worked for F S Ratcliffe and Sons, now known as Robert Riley Ltd, where I am a director. At that time, I knew that the way to make money was to run your own business, and I wanted it to be in manufacturing.

So in 1963 I left Ratcliffe to start Smith Springs (Rochdale) Ltd. While I knew about sales, I had a colleague who understood manufacturing. We were backed by four local businessmen. There were just the two of us, some second-hand machinery and a small lock-up that we paid £5 a week rent for.

The mistake I made came early on. It was all to do with an order we got for two springs from Pilkington's Glass in St Helens. Three or four months after the business had started I went to St Helens to see Pilkingtons to try and get more business.

'Now then, so you think you can make springs?' said the buyer when I got there. 'Yes', I said. 'Well, you'd better come and have a look at this one, then,' he said, and took me out into the factory to look at it. It was massive. It was a coil spring – just like a spring in a clock – only it was about four foot in diameter. 'Could you make one of these?' he asked.

I said that I wasn't certain, but thought that we could.

'I'll tell you what, then,' he said, 'put it in your car, take it back to the factory, work out if you can make it, and let me have me a quote.' Well,

I thought, this is alright. So I took it back to the works, and showed it to the technical man. 'Can we make these?' I asked. He said that he thought that we could, and so I worked out a price.

It was a good price – because we were only a small firm, and wanted to win orders, especially from a big company like Pilkingtons. It came to £150 for the two springs – £75 a piece. So I telephoned the buyer back, and said yes, we could make them, and it would cost them £150. 'Right then,' he said. 'So that's £300 for the two. I'll send you the order in tonight's post.' Well, I was amazed. There's more money in springs than meets the eye, I thought.

When we got the order we set about buying the material to make them. For these particular springs, we needed steel in 156 foot lengths. There was only one problem: 23 foot was the longest length that we could buy in the size that we needed. We searched high and low, even trying companies in Sweden and Germany. We couldn't get it anywhere.

But we weren't going to give up – not with the carrot dangling in front of us of more work from Pilkingtons. We scratched our heads and eventually decided that we'd just have to get ourselves out of the mess that we were in. So we wound up making the springs by welding seven of the 23 foot lengths together, whilst they were red-hot, and coiling them on a lathe whilst they were still glowing.

So there we are. Is that one mistake or two? To begin with, I didn't quote the right price: Pilkingtons were quite ready to pay twice as much as I was asking.

Second, I had been rather rash in accepting the order before I was even sure whether we could make the springs. I should have anticipated that there would be a snag. Still, we did make the springs in the end and I learnt two business lessons that I never forgot.

31 March 1991

Lord Delfont

Lord Delfont, 82, is chairman of First Leisure Corporation with a 4 per cent shareholding. He grew up in the East End, and became an agent and impresario, establishing stars such as Norman Wisdom and Morcambe and Wise. For more than 25 years he presented the Royal Variety Performance, and after joining his brothers Lew and Leslie in the Grade Organization, masterminded the sale of the company to EMI. When Thorn EMI's leisure division was bought by Trust House Forte he moved with the company, and two years later led one of the biggest buy-outs in City history.

My biggest mistake was probably turning down the chance to manage the Beatles, though it was not the only time I turned down something that went on to be phenomenally successful.

In February 1963 I was looking for a popular group to put in the Royal Variety Performance. My daughter Susan said: 'Daddy, why don't you put the Beatles in?' I said I had never heard of them.

When I got back to the office I discovered that they were doing a concert for us at the Princess Theatre in Torquay the following Sunday. So I rang to find out how the bookings were doing. Apparently people were sleeping in the streets waiting for ticket returns. That was good enough for me, so I booked them for the Royal Variety Performance in November.

A short time later Brian Epstein came round to the office to ask if we would like to manage the Beatles with him. One of my chaps said: 'Well, what do they want?' He mentioned something like £750 a week and we thought that was outrageous, so we turned them down. But their popularity just grew and grew and come the Royal Variety Performance they were a world-wide phenomenon.

I shall never understand why I said no. We had nothing to lose by taking them on. It wasn't as if we couldn't afford it. And we could have made an awful lot of money. But you couldn't have predicted just how big the Beatles were to become. That kind of success simply hadn't been seen before, and back in the spring of 1963 it had yet to become apparent.

I suppose in lost opportunity it cost us about £10m. I learnt from the experience never to write people off. Even if an artist goes through a bad period, I say: 'Well, it doesn't matter . . . they'll come back.'

In 1968, I turned down the musical *Hair!* because I didn't like the language. I heard the record. There were lots of 'f's in it, and things. Maybe I was being old-fashioned, but I thought: 'That's not for me.' The show, of course, went on to be a world-wide success.

And again, when I was with EMI, I turned down Monty Python's *Life of Brian*. I gave them a £50,000 advance – we were due to invest about £2m – but when I got the script I felt it was blasphemous and decided not to go ahead.

When it opened, I went along to see what they had done with it, and I found they had changed it quite a lot. But this is why, as the credits are rolling at the end of the film, Eric Idle says: 'I told them, Bernie. I said,"It'll never make money."'

Brian was another huge success. I remember George Harrison coming up and shaking my hand on the plane back from New York. He thanked me for turning it down because it enabled his company, Handmade Films, to produce it. Those three mistakes probably cost about £30m, but I have never worried about setbacks. You can't expect everything to go the way you want it, and there is always something else around the corner.

If you're in the theatre or film business, you've got to be emotionally involved with whatever you do. You can't look at something and say: 'Well, I don't like it, but I'm sure it will make money.' You have to trust your own judgement. I've only ever done things I like, even if I know they won't make money. Therefore, I have no regrets. And I've learnt that making mistakes hasn't really hurt me in the least.

21 April 1991

Creenagh Lodge

Creenagh Lodge, 49, is chairman of Craton Lodge & Knight, the new-product development and marketing company, which she helped found in 1972. She and her fellow board members decided to enter the Soviet market at what turned out to be a terrible cost to the company, ending in a financial restructuring of the group. After graduating from Cambridge with a degree in social anthropology she went into market research and has 20 years of experience of all aspects of product and brand development. She is expert in adapting successful brands for foreign markets.

I would say that my biggest mistake, along with the rest of my board at Craton Lodge & Knight, was also a very gallant, interesting and worthy mistake. Like Napoleon we were defeated by the very great difficulty of getting Russia to change.

Back in 1986 we decided to expand the business into the Soviet Union. It was in the early, exciting days of Gorbachev, *glasnost* and *perestroika*. We knew the Soviets needed to sell their goods to the West, and we also knew there was a very strong wish to learn Western skills in computing, marketing and product development. With our experience we felt this represented a great opportunity.

We were lucky enough to have someone who was familiar with the Soviet Union's culture and commerce. We set up a venture with a newly-created Moscow publicity agency, Vneshtorgraklama. A Soviet trainee in marketing was sent over to work in our office and we set up a unit with Russian speakers at our head office.

We started looking at several manufacturing enterprises that wanted to know about Western markets and to develop goods for those countries. I got quite excited, because there seemed to be considerable potential. These enterprises had products which could be amended and sold to the West. But at every turn we were defeated by Gosplan, the state planning agency, which prevented us from making the necessary changes.

As soon as we realized it was going to be extremely difficult, if not impossible, to get products moving out of the Soviet Union to the West, we turned our attention to bringing Western goods and marketing techniques into the Soviet Union.

We did quite a lot of work and were involved in a whole range of exciting plans for conference centres and the introduction of marketing skills. We were also working with other Western organizations which were keen to establish productive working relationships with the Soviets.

The problem was that the Soviets simply wouldn't, or couldn't, pay. They played for time, then they would pick holes in the contracts that they themselves had helped write. Our best endeavours came to nothing and we found the cost was too high. It wasn't simply the direct cost of the investment, it was also the time needed to get to know a fundamentally different cultural and manufacturing set-up.

Finally, our Russian unit suffered a cash crisis. Earnings were too small and too late and the unit was eating up capital. We were by now much more interested in Europe and were not prepared to go on funding the Russian enterprise. We stayed until 1990, hoping that it would come good. But in the end we were forced to sell it. We ran into cash-flow problems with the group as a whole and in March 1990 we sold off not only the Russian unit but also three other companies. The group had to be restructured and we returned to our core business.

I learned two lessons. One was that we were too small in financial terms to withstand the long haul required in the Soviet Union. The second was that our expertise in Europe offered the most profitable way forward. If we had pulled the Russian venture off, everyone would have hailed us as visionaries. Happily our investment in and understanding of Europe is paying off handsomely and, who knows, as Eastern Europe moves towards the West the day might come when we find ourselves back there again.

28 April 1991

Sir Graham Day

Sir Graham Day wanted to be a baritone singer. Instead he became chairman of the Rover Group, Cadbury Schweppes, PowerGen and Crombie Insurance (UK). Born in Novia Scotia (in 1933), he studied law, eventually joining the old railroad company, Canadian Pacific. In 1971 he came to the UK to sort problems at the Cammell Laird shipyard. Acquiring a reputation as a management troubleshooter, he went on to run British Shipbuilders and then Rover Group in 1986. He is also deputy chairman of MAI, and a director of BAe, the Laird Group and Thorn EMI.

My biggest mistake was accepting a government appointment as deputy chairman and chief executive of the organizing committee for British Shipbuilders. It was an absolute fiasco.

To set the background, in 1970 I was working for Canadian Pacific as general solicitor. If a wheel fell off somewhere in the world, I would be sent to try and put it back on. We had ordered three container ships from Cammell Laird Shipbuilders, but in 1970 the company was going bust. I came to Britain to try and make sure that our ships were delivered.

A year later I was asked to run Cammell Laird. My father was British and England had always appealed to me, so I said yes. It was a happy time because we started to produce a profit, employment stabilized and orders started to come in.

Towards the end of 1975 the Labour Government asked me to become the chief executive of what was to be British Shipbuilders. Putting politics and personal concern aside, I thought that nationalization might provide the framework within which British shipbuilding might be preserved. So in a weak moment I accepted the job. And that was a mistake which still haunts me. What Labour had in me was someone with value as a manager. What they wanted was a gofer, an administrator who did what he was told. 1976 really was the worst working year of my life.

I remember telling ministers that they had to come clean with everybody – unions and management. If we moved quickly we could restructure and save more than if we just let it slide. But I was told it was just another cyclical downturn and I was being a little emotional.

At this time Labour had a paper-thin majority in the Commons, and on 27 November 1976 the bill to nationalize the industry failed. Incidentally, that's the day I stopped shaving. The beard has been with me ever since.

Quite by accident, however, I had managed to get one thing right. My contract legally died with the bill, so in effect I was no longer employed. I didn't walk out, I just declined to renew the contract.

The industry was nationalized the following year, and of course it went downhill because you couldn't cure its problems simply by throwing pound notes at it. In my view, the shipbuilding industry we have in Britain today is very much smaller than it would have been had the critical decisions been taken in 1976.

And it demonstrated to my total and abiding satisfaction that whether you use Labour-style nationalization or not, one thing government is guaranteed to do worse than anybody else is manage any commercial operation.

In the end, everybody got hit by the shipbuilding crisis. But those who restructured – like Germany – survived in better shape. The UK just let it all happen, and tens of thousands of people lost their jobs as a result.

There was nothing I could do about it, and that was why taking that job was an appalling personal decision. I was totally frustrated. I had no authority.

In 1983, I came back to try and salvage what was left of British Shipbuilders. It meant closing down anything that couldn't be saved, and it was not a pleasant job. I was doing things that should have been done in 1976.

The whole thing was a frightening experience. But it has made me a much better manager. I take a lot less on faith now. Being sceptical is not such a bad attribute.

5 May 1991

Peter Revell-Smith

Peter Revell-Smith, 66, is chairman of the board of governors of the Museum of London. After Winchester and a spell in the war with the Coldstream Guards he went to McGill University in Canada and then Columbia University in New York. On his return to the UK he joined Unilever as a management trainee before moving to the City in 1956 to become an investment banker. He went on to manage various quoted companies in the UK and abroad. He is now a member of the Court of Common Council, a governor of the City University and a director of the City Polytechnic.

My biggest mistake was a triumph of enthusiasm over good judgement. It happened in my twenty-fifth summer which I spent travelling in the US.

I had been in the war, and just graduated in commerce from McGill in Canada. I was due at Columbia University in New York in the autumn to study for an MSc. In the meantime, I set off with three friends in a beaten-up old car to drive to Los Angeles.

We were sleeping out because we had so little money and couldn't afford to stay anywhere. But when we reached Los Angeles I was put in touch with an extraordinary, elderly lady, the daughter of Mr Colgate of dental fame. I worked for her for six weeks earning $150 a week, which was jolly good money in those days.

With my capital of $900 I joined my friends in Mexico City. There I saw these spectacularly lovely onyx things – ash trays, cigarette boxes, lighters, bookends, that sort of thing. Here's an opportunity, I thought. I arranged with the others to buy up onyx as cheaply as possible and ship it to me in New York. I offered them a cut, enough to ensure they would be sufficiently interested to do their best on my behalf, and left them with $250.

This was enough to purchase a packing-case-full of onyx. When it arrived at my hall of residence, 10 per cent of the stuff was broken, and the box only fitted in my room if I left the door open.

I looked up department stores in the telephone directory and set off with my samples. Almost the first buyer I visited, at Lord & Taylor, said the things were lovely and took the lot for $500.

I was paid within the week and, thinking I was brilliant, sent the $500 straight down to Mexico with an order for two more cases of onyx. Several days later I thought I'd go and see how the things were moving at Lord & Taylor. To my horror it was quite obvious that they weren't moving at all. The store had added their own big mark up and I suppose the public thought it was too expensive. But I was irrevocably committed to the next shipment, which duly arrived after two and a half weeks.

By now I had learnt two fundamental business lessons. First and foremost, if you want to sell things, see if people are buying them before you order more. The second is that to double up with your only remaining capital is, to put it mildly, rather risky. Essentially you are playing double or quits. Whilst the two new cases were on their way to New York I received a summons from the buyer at Lord & Taylor. She was a pretty tough character and I didn't need to be a genius to know what she was going to say. She wanted me to take my onyx back, but of course I had no money and couldn't. As you might imagine we didn't part on very good terms.

I hadn't grasped that Lord & Taylor was pretty up-market. It had really been luck – as it happened rather unfortunate luck – that they had ordered straight away. But I couldn't repeat it anywhere else. I started going down-market, but that didn't work either.

I descended to hawking the stuff around various tobacconists at a much-reduced price. It was hard work since the stuff was so heavy and I only managed to sell half a case. In the end I left the remainder with a friend to sell if he could since I was coming back to this country.

What was really galling is that it wasn't as if I was a callow youth. But I learned that the theory of economics and commerce, and putting them into practice, are very different.

12 May 1991

Michael Peters

Michael Peters headed the first design company to be floated on the Stock Exchange. He graduated from the London College of Printing before obtaining a masters in fine arts at Yale University. In 1970 he formed design consultancy Michael Peters and Partners. After ambitious expansion sent it into receivership he returned to basics with Michael Peters Ltd.

My biggest mistake was expanding outside our normal area of activity in businesses we did not know enough about.

The company had grown with a tremendous track record in brand and corporate identity, designing everything from packaging, annual reports, and identities for clients such as PowerGen.

We floated the business in 1983 to give our 60 employees a stake in it at a reasonable price. For two or three years we were very much the darlings of the stock market. It was only when we were tempted to expand our business that we went wrong.

Towards the end of 1985, we got involved in retail design, exhibitions and conference presentation. Then it was human resource management, event management . . . everything we felt our clients could possibly need. Some of the companies we bought were very successful, others were not. So the first mistake was to look for areas of related opportunity rather than expand our own core business.

It's a common story, but, lured by the money that was thrown at us, we expanded far too quickly. We did not think as carefully as we should have done about clients' future requirements. We moved from areas of business that were very profitable to others that we didn't truly understand. We felt that our clients needed those services and, indeed, many did take advantage of them. It wasn't just a mad whim. We wanted to expand by acquiring like-minded businesses and the companies we bought to work together to help our clients.

But at the end of the day, trying to make our management team, which had been used to working in the brand and corporate identity business, manage activities it wasn't familiar with was a recipe for disaster.

Although we were successful with our business, things went disastrously wrong when at the end of 1988 we expanded into a market that has been the graveyard for many a company – North America.

With such a good reputation in the European market, we felt we could export that 'Europeanness' to the US. We bought several companies; one specialized in designing large stores such as Bloomingdales, another marketed events. Our packaging, brand, and corporate identity business in New York and Toronto went very well indeed. But America is a different world, and it's very difficult to control what goes on 3,500 miles away. I worked there for six months, but quite honestly, trying to cope with running an international business and a small management team with such diverse business interest was very difficult.

And, of course, the inevitable happened. We got hit by bad debts in North America, the marketing services industry collapsed and the recession moved into the UK. Not surprisingly, the Michael Peters Group got into difficulty. Today, we are back to running our core business as Michael Peters Ltd. We are working fiercely in the European market, just as we always did before. We are once again back to basics, working with those clients who have always worked with us in our core brand and corporate identity business. That's what made us famous in the first place, and that's where we made our money. It has been a very painful experience, but I've learnt a big lesson. From now on, we'll be sticking firmly to what we know best, what gives us most pleasure and what gives our clients the best creative and financial results.

2 June 1991

Quentin Bell

> Quentin Bell, 46, runs one of the UK's top ten independent public relations agencies. He was born in Reading and, he says, did not have much education. He started his career on a local newspaper in Reading and then moved to Thompson Newspapers as a trainee reporter. He joined Haymarket Publishing and then went on to become marketing director of a small tour operator, before embarking on a career in public relations. In 1973, he started the Quentin Bell Organization. His first book, *The PR Business*, was published by Kogan Page in March 1992.

I made my biggest mistake in 1976, only three years after starting my company. It was a sharp lesson in flit management; the art of veering from one idea to another without doing either of them well.

We were looking for something different to raise the profile of one of our clients, an upmarket menswear shop in South Molton Street. Suddenly I had what I thought was a brilliant idea. I suggested they sold their own perfume, a unique male fragrance created specially for them.

We did our research and discovered that the perfume business is all about image, packaging and branding. The product itself, provided it doesn't smell like a skunk, is actually almost irrelevant.

It may sound stupid, but that to me was an amazing revelation. Perfume is the ultimate exercise in marketing, and I felt that if I could go to magazines like *Vogue* and announce the launch of an exclusive male fragrance it would provide a hook on which to hang the promotion of the whole shop. However, the retailer didn't share my vision and declined to take up the idea. So I decided there were lots of other upmarket boutiques around the country and I could sell it to them instead.

I formed a company and had three or four fragrances made up. Next, I devised a wonderfully complex system whereby each store could dispense the perfume from a Russian tea urn. The labels said 'Samovar from . . . ' with the name of the shop printed on.

I imported samovars from the Soviet Union which had to be specially fitted up. It was very expensive. I then hit on the idea of having personalized labels on the other side of each bottle so it would make an exclusive gift. I got the 100 most popular male and female Christian names processed and gave each store a kit.

At first the idea went down very well, but retailers who had loved the concept when I sold it to them soon realized they had to have these bloody tea urns sitting around. They were complicated to deal with and often got knocked over. In the end I decided enough was enough and got out. In total, I must have invested around £50,000, which was a lot of money for a young company. But it was a great mistake to learn from. Trying to get it off the ground had taken up 70 per cent of my time. I was trying to develop another business while my staff looked after our existing clients with my strategic overview. It sounded great in theory, but in practice I was giving far too much attention to something that turned out to be peripheral.

It had taken my eye off the ball of the Quentin Bell Organization, and I had lost the original South Molton Street client as a result. In reality, I had been running with a mad idea that had totally consumed me for a while. For a start, the whole business was far too complicated anyway; ever since, I have kept things simple. And relying on outsiders to dispense the product into bottles was a big mistake, because it meant I wasn't in control. Having learnt my lesson I went on to build QBO fairly successfully. And we've grown at a steady rate of up to 30 per cent a year as a result. We decided not to expand the business abroad, instead concentrating on providing a quality service here. We know what we are best at and we make a good profit.

But if you know anyone who wants to buy a couple of hundred bottles of perfume, they're still sitting in the shed. I kept them as a reminder not to diversify too fast.

9 June 1991

Eric Verdon-Roe

Eric Verdon-Roe, 38, is managing director of EVRO Publishing, a company he owns jointly with Haymarket Publishing, and of Haymarket Specialist Motoring Magazines. He joined Haymarket as a sales representative in 1976 after reading geography at Exeter University. Believing him unemployable, his father had bet him £100 he could not get a job within 24 hours. He replied to the first advertisement he saw, insisted on being intereviewed immediately and started work soon after. Although he only intended to work a couple of days to collect on the bet, he has stayed for fifteen years.

My biggest mistake was in 1983, when I launched a specialist health magazine which was ahead of its time.

Haymarket has traditionally published trade and male interest magazines, but we were looking for new markets and new opportunities. Up until then, health had always been an incredibly cranky thing, pill-popping . . . open-toe sandals . . . California culture, that sort of stuff.

But healthy living and fitness were obviously going to be two of the big things of the 1980s, so we decided to launch a specialist magazine called *New Health*, which at the time was very different from anything else that was available.

For about eighteen months the response was extremely good. We had identified something which became much bigger than we had ever contemplated, but this brought its own set of problems.

It was the subject's very success that was to be our downfall. First, the health pages of magazines like *Cosmopolitan* and *Options* started to adopt very similar styles, then whole publications cottoned on to what we were doing. As a consequence, we had become almost a trade magazine and everyone else was creaming off the glitz. They adopted the bits they liked and cashed in on it.

And the frustration for me was that I found all my advertisers would rather have the glitz than the real stuff. We wanted to be carrying major supermarket advertisements for products like low-fat yoghurts, but the politics of food is just amazing.

The problem was that I had editorial staff who were pointing out that despite the labelling, the food inside was the same old rubbish as before.

And we actually alienated our advertisers by telling the truth. Our campaigning journalism won a lot of awards. And there were lots of scare stories from which we got enormous publicity, which put even more advertisers off.

I learnt a lot of lessons, all of which seem obvious now. First, we were trying to invent something, and that is not the role of a specialist magazine. Pioneering is for TV, radio and newspapers. Magazines are for hobbies, and should therefore pick up on trends, not try to create them. Second, we were selling bad news and that was another mistake. Your average person wants to read good news and promises about how to lose weight, and so on.

As the advertisers slipped away, we fell into the clutches of the very people we were trying to get away from – those wonderful producers of green-lipped mussel extract, ginseng and garlic pearl capsules. But towards the end I was grateful even for them, because I'd seen all my other advertisers, my staff and my ideas disappearing off in other directions.

We found ourselves left with a magazine that had pioneered a marketplace which then moved away from us. Eventually, we paid the bills and pulled the plug.

Even now, I see a lot of publishers who get frustrated because they've got a brilliant product and can't understand why it doesn't sell. They think somehow it's unfair. But the fact is, if the public doesn't want to buy it, then it's not a brilliant product. Ever since, I have been much less idealistic. I don't think magazine publishing and idealism go hand in hand. But I don't have any regrets, because I learnt an awful lot – more than I have learnt from more successful launches, either subsequently or before.

14 July 1991

Stephen Franklin

Stephen Franklin, 43, is managing director of Commodore Business Machines (UK). After taking a degree in Spanish at the University of Madrid, he started selling photocopying machines for Rank Xerox. Having become UK sales manager of the advanced systems division, he joined Granada as head of the business centres initiative, marketing computer corporate systems solutions. He took up his current position in 1987. Commodore, which then had a £15.5m UK turnover, has increased this by 450 per cent and claims it is the world's biggest shipper of PCs.

My biggest mistake was trying to sell home computer packages containing non-computer-related products.

Our packages came complete with machine, joystick and software. They were very successful until 1989, when we had what we thought was a brilliant idea.

British Airways was giving huge publicity to Air Miles, and we decided to do a summer package for £499. We put an Amiga 500 computer together with some software and 500 Air Miles; enough for a flight to Paris or Amsterdam. We bought enough for 25,000 packages, and we spent about £100,000 on advertising. It was a disaster; I think we sold 5,000 in total. We had spent about £120,000 on Air Miles, which we couldn't do anything with. Our contract only applied to home computers; anything else would have interfered with other dealers.

Next, we put together 25,000 Home Entertainment packs for Christmas. They included the C64 computer, games, a personal stereo and a guitar synthesizer, all for £199. It was another disaster; we sold about 7,000.

Fortunately, when the Berlin Wall came down the first thing they wanted to buy was personal stereos. There was a great shortage, so we managed to get rid of them. But I was left with about 18,000 guitar synthesizers, which I ended up selling on to a wholesaler.

Last year we made another mistake. We decided that if we wanted to keep the low end of the market, we ought to bring out a console. This was a very grave error.

Consoles don't use cassettes or discs and they don't have a keyboard; all you can do is play games. We were under a bit of pressure because consoles have taken off in America; Nintendo has sold something like 33 million. So we took our C64 computer, designed a plastic mould round it to look like a console, and manufactured 80,000 for the UK market, retailing at £99. We spent £150,000 on marketing, and again it was absolutely disastrous; we sold about 15,000.

Until then, we had sold millions of the C64 complete with keyboard for £149. I think what happened was that dealers and shopkeepers said: 'Why pay £99 when all you can do is play games? Why not spend £149 and have a computer as well?' As a result, our sales of the C64 were up 40 per cent on the year before, so it wasn't a total disaster. But it was a very expensive lesson.

Our business is selling home computers, not consoles. And this year our sales of peripherals are up by about 400 per cent, which means people are doing a lot more than just playing games. So we won't be entering the console market in the UK. The games are more expensive and there is no educational benefit.

Those three mistakes were pretty bad, and there are no excuses. I just had to say to my bosses in America: 'I'm sorry, we cocked up in the UK.' But we learnt a lot. First, if you're trying to sell a computer, just because everybody is jumping on the bandwagon of a new promotion scheme don't automatically assume it will work for you. We used to sit around saying, 'This seems to be the flavour of the month, let's give it a try,' when we should have been asking 'Is this what the end-user wants?' We now know that if you include non-computer-related products in a package, it will be a disaster. All of our other packages have been phenomenally successful, and that is how we have increased our sales.

24 July 1991

Anita Roddick

Anita Roddick, 48, is founder and managing director of the Body Shop. She trained as a teacher at Bath College and worked for the United Nations in Geneva before opening the first Body Shop in 1976 with a loan of £4,000. In 1984 the company went public, and today it has an annual turnover of £84.5m, with more than 600 shops trading in 40 countries. Roddick was Businesswoman of the Year in 1985, given an OBE in 1988, and received a United Nations environmental award in 1989. Her book, *Body and Soul*, was published in September 1991.

The biggest mistake I ever made was using sophisticated imagery to try and get a simple message across to the public.

In 1987, we were campaigning on behalf of Friends of the Earth. They had an advertising agency to organize the design for our windows; and we had agreed to print the leaflets, talk about acid rain and get millions of new members for them.

The advertising agency found an extraordinary Polish artist, who produced a surreal poster showing a dead tree sprouting from a decomposing human head against an industrial background of smoking chimneys. The copyline said 'Acid Reign', which we thought was really clever. And we put dead branches in the windows to go with the posters.

The trouble was, the public hadn't a clue what we were getting at. On the very first day, a customer walked in and said: 'You've spelt rain wrong.' Then another one came in and said: 'How much are the dried branches? What are you supposed to do with them?' Someone else asked if we were selling LSD.

This happened in every shop, and we suddenly realized that people didn't understand. The posters had gone up, we'd printed a couple of hundred thousand leaflets, and all we'd achieved was to mystify everybody. We'd got it absolutely wrong. And Friends of the Earth gained less than 500 new members. It was arrogance on our part, because we just hadn't related to the public. They didn't want sophisticated complex images. They wanted simplicity.

We hadn't thought about what was right for them, what was easiest. And no matter how much you love the cause, if you can't communicate you might as well just not be there.

We've conducted about eight campaigns with Friends of the Earth since then. But we have insisted on doing our own designs, so that the imagery is relevant to the people who come into the shops. It has worked. And so my secret love affair with advertising agencies got kicked into reality. There is no feedback loop with ads. That's the element that was missing; it was a monologue, it's never a dialogue.

We know our customers. We know how to humanize a cause, we know how to make an image simple.

In the past, we tended to be seduced by other people's knowledge, because there are no books telling you how to deal with a company growth rate of 50 per cent a year. But each time we've worked with consultants, we've been bitterly disappointed. We always wanted to hear advice and we were thrilled if anyone agreed with what we were doing, but it rarely happened.

The experience with the advertising agency was an immense lesson, and we then started to look at the role of consultants. We had used them for computer technology, for recruitment – but nothing they did ever seemed right. They had so little understanding of our style, image and needs. It started our belief that we should never work with anybody else, just do what we do and do it better.

The Body Shop is my business: I work here, and I know it better than anybody else. I suddenly realized that outside consultants' advice is like the smallest-denomination coin – of little value. We know what our customers want, because we ask them.

In the end, the best advert is a good product, a good shop, staff that are thrilled by what you do, and customers not hyped out or overmarketed or overwhelmed by advertising.

8 September 1991

John Bintliff

John Bintliff, 42, is non-executive chairman of Elan, the UK overnight delivery company. He is also group marketing director of Eyetech Group, the leading supplier of information systems to the transport and distribution industry. Bintliff spent seventeen years with the Post Office after taking a degree in economics and law at Cambridge. He became deputy marketing director at Royal Mail Parcelforce, then in 1989 became sales and marketing director at Securicor. In February, he joined Eyetech, which was recently called in by DHL to run Elan, pending sale negotiations.

My biggest mistake was working in the public sector for too long. In 1970, when I left Cambridge, I judged companies that I wanted to join very much on the way in which they treated me during the interview. The Post Office gave me the most thorough going-over I've ever had in my life.

After two days of constant tests, I was very impressed by the way in which they seemed to be aiming to become a commercial organization. I believed, and perhaps fell for, their PR activity. I felt they were going to be quite separate from government.

Of the ten locations where they had jobs for management trainees, I was asked where I would most and least like to go. I said I would most like to go to Bristol, and least like to go to Manchester.

So I spent two-and-a-half years in Manchester as assistant postal controller before being promoted to Central Audit in London. My function was to try to stop people from making entrepreneurial decisions and get them to work to set patterns. I was moved into pay and grading for a while. Then I became personal assistant to the managing director.

When British Telecom was launched, the Post Office slipped back into its rut of being a quasi-civil service department. I became PA to the chairman, Sir Ronald Dearing, and after a few months he said it was about time I did a real job.

So I became deputy postmaster of southeast London, going from a staff of seventeen to one of nearly 6,000. On the very first day, all 38 union branches gathered to present me with a problem they'd been trying to solve for twelve years.

At last, after a total of fifteen years, my talents in marketing were identified, and I went on to what became Parcelforce. I had a series of jobs launching new products, finally becoming deputy marketing director. I would have had a long and secure career with the Post Office, but my entrepreneurial skills were not being used to the full. I realized it was time to move on.

In 1989, I became sales and marketing director of Securicor and during my time there relaunched it as Omega Express. But I still felt I was in a quasi-public organization, so I joined Eyetech.

In retrospect, I wish I had moved into the private sector four years earlier. I reckon it cost me about half a million pounds. The public sector is a wonderful training ground in which to try out your ideas. You can make some rather huge mistakes and get away with them – that would never happen in the private sector. But you spend too much time on bureaucracy and the inevitable fights between divisions.

Moving into the private sector has taught me the importance of keeping in touch with the customer, remembering that he is king and you should respond to his wishes. In a smaller company you can execute change far more quickly, and you get far more satisfaction.

I don't want to knock the Post Office, but for a long time they believed everybody could do everything, and people found themselves in areas they weren't very good at.

By contrast, I now firmly believe you have to specialize before you can be a good general manager. In the private sector, you can exploit your talents. The moral is, you should realize when you are in a rut, and take action more quickly than I did. Frankly, you should seek opportunities to get involved with the private sector as early as you possibly can.

29 September 1991

William Sargent

William Sargent, 35, is chairman of Spitting Image Productions and managing director of Viva Pictures. He became a financier in the television industry after taking a degree in business and legal studies at Trinity College, Dublin. In 1985 he founded the Frame Store, one of London's leading digital video post-production facilities. Over the last two years he has put together more than £15m of funding for European programming, and acted as executive producer on Prix Italia winners and British Academy nominees. He is currently making a film of Bruce Chatwin's novel *Utz*.

My biggest mistake was trying to do business on the strength of a handshake without doing enough research first.

In 1983, I had just sold a company which distributed video equipment around Europe, and I was looking for new opportunities. Quite idealistically, I decided I should be trying to put something back into Ireland, where I come from.

I had run three businesses while I was at college to pay for my education, so I knew my way around. And over the next two years, I attempted to set up three partnerships. On each occasion I did so without a contract. It cost me around £100,000.

The first two cases involved importing various video-related goods. On both occasions they refused to pay the agreed price on delivery. Both sets of people reckoned they could renegotiate the package because the goods were already in the country. And because I had paid the freight bills to get them there, I didn't really have the option of shipping them back out again.

On the third attempt, the problem was that both the people selling the equipment, and the potential customers, were never honest with us in terms of their ability to deliver and their ability to pay. Instead of a business, we had a number of people saying they could do things which they couldn't, and at the point when I owed £40,000 to the Irish banks, I called it a day.

I paid the money back, but as a result, when we started the Frame Store, my wife and I didn't have the capital to take a big enough stake. It went on to become one of the most successful companies in the industry, and in order to own the stake we deserved, we really had to pay for it.

Funnily enough, I still do business on a handshake.

I never want to go into a business on my own; I always look for a partner. I have neither the aptitude nor the desire to run a business on a day-to-day level. I work as a strategist, identifying opportunities and creating relationships, preferably in niche markets.

If you're going to make money in the long term, you've got to stick with someone you trust, because you don't control the chequebook and therefore you can be fiddled.

After five years it could cost you substantial amounts of money, so you might as well find out in the first twelve months if that trust is going to be betrayed.

Trying to enforce contracts only creates ulcers; it's virtually impossible. If, instead, you recognize that you're never going to get what you set out to get or that you made a mistake, you save yourself a lot of angst. On that basis, I decided quite early on that I would try to do business with people on trust. Most times it works, but in Ireland it was a complete failure.

The Germans and the Japanese understand long-term partnerships. They're not in it for this year's deal. That is the reason for doing business on a handshake. It is an incentive for the person to mislead you; so you find out in time that you shouldn't be in partnership.

No one person has all the skills to create a successful business. It has to be a team effort. I will not attempt again to do business in Ireland, but I've learnt to spend a lot more time on research before entering a partnership.

You have to be partners in spirit, not in contract. And if the partnership can't be based on a handshake, then when the pressure is on, your business will fall apart.

20 October 1991

Nicholas Jenkins

Nicholas Jenkins, 52, is chairman and corporate design director of The Jenkins Group. After leaving St Martin's School of Art, he spent ten years as a freelance designer. During that time he was also a senior tutor at the Royal College of Art and guest lecturer at Yale University. In 1972, he founded the Jenkins Group. Clients have included W H Smith, the Arts Council and the Commonwealth Development Corporation. Current projects include Victoria Coach Station and Docklands Light Railway. His latest book – *The Business of Image* – is published by Kogan Page.

My biggest mistake was not taking more executive control when I first started the company in 1972. I had landed a minor contract to redesign the corporate identity for W H Smith. It was patently impossible to do that on my own, so I had to employ people.

Running a business was never one of my ambitions, and I decided, rather selfishly, that I would sit at my drawing board, be the creative director, and let somebody else worry about the rest.

At first the company developed successfully along the lines I intended. In other words, it was design led, it produced work we thought was very good. The clients appeared satisfied, and everything was going very well. But when we got to a certain size, it became necessary to appoint a managing director. However, by doing that the culture of the company had to change – we became more business oriented.

Our major corporate identity projects were for retail organizations, and we got a reputation for being retail designers.

In fact, we were corporate identity designers. But since we had this strange reputation, we decided to stick with it. That meant employing specialist retail designers. So we pinched some very good people from rival companies. The company continued to grow quickly, and by the late 1980s we employed about 75. We had a marketing department of seventeen, which is a really grotesque proportion for a design consultancy.

The problem was that we had become obsessed with growth. We were no longer design led; we were business led. We even seriously discussed the notion of going on the Unlisted Securities Market. But perhaps that was our best failure. We were so busy expanding we couldn't even put in the management time necessary.

I have nothing against good business practices, but if they overtake the product, then they are self-defeating.

Eventually the cultural disagreements between the managing director, the retail design director and myself became untenable, and they decided to leave.

The next problem was our size, which I had allowed to get out of hand. When the recession came along, retail design disappeared, and I was stuck with an enormous company including seventeen marketing people with nobody to sell to. I had to make people redundant, which was the worst thing I have ever had to do.

However, we have struggled through and emerged in much better shape. We have returned to the original values and I feel very happy about that. I find myself in an extremely good position at the moment. I'm back on the drawing board, which is what I'm best at, but I have taken on the responsibility of chairman quite willingly this time.

I've learnt a lot about how to run a company, and I have a managing director who is in total sympathy with what we are doing.

Corporate identity design is the largest part of our business, but we've carved a new niche as a result of the demise of retail design. We're doing fantastic projects that really fascinate me because they're a true marriage of interior and graphic design.

So in a sense, the whole business throughout this traumatic period has reverted to something that I wanted in the first place.

The moral is, you've got to keep your eye absolutely on what it is that you want to do. Peripheral considerations just for the sake of growth are extremely dangerous.

10 November 1991

John Beckwith

John Beckwith, 44, is chairman and chief executive of London & Edinburgh Trust, one of the UK's leading property groups. He was educated at Harrow and became the headmaster of a prep school in Maidstone at the age of eighteen. In 1968 he joined Arthur Andersen, where he practised accountancy for four years prior to forming LET with his brother Peter in 1971. In April 1990 the company was sold to the Swedish insurance group SPP for £510m. Its property portfolio and development programme is spread throughout Europe, the US, Hong Kong and Singapore.

My biggest mistake was a combination of diversifying into areas we knew nothing about and backing entrepreneurs with little to lose themselves. After the property crash in 1974, there were no developments to do. It wasn't a question of wanting to diversify, we had to, because the company had to be kept afloat.

The banks were still lending us money, so we had the wherewithal to back small businesses. That was another mistake. We had listened to our bank manager and had accepted the money. But we had not thought about the pitfalls.

So we sold engines to Australia, shipped Range Rovers to Iran and traded in Bedford trucks. In the last case, we lost a lot of money. We put a deposit down with some lawyers, who were meant to keep it until the trucks were delivered, but they handed it over to the suppliers, who then did a bunk.

Which just goes to prove you shouldn't trust anybody – not even solicitors. Next we imported 45,000 pairs of boots from Brazil and opened a letter of credit with the Central Bank of Nigeria. We planned to sell the boots to the Nigerian army. But when we opened the first container it was full of left-footed boots. The second container was exactly the same, so was the third.

The bank honoured the letter of credit, so we can only assume that the next lot of containers – which we hadn't dared open – contained the right-footed boots. Either that or the Nigerian army was running round with two left feet for a few years.

We also bought a sausage-making factory in Cornwall which had a contract to supply the Royal Navy. But most of the sausages seemed to be disappearing elsewhere and we weren't being paid, so that business had to be sold. Next we had a couple of furniture companies. One was very successful, the other wasn't. The delivery vans were arriving on Saturdays when the factory was meant to be closed, and the product was going out of the back door.

Then I backed a couple of entrepreneurs who had a contract with one of the biggest ski manufacturers. Again, I made the mistake of not making sure they had enough money to lose themselves. They didn't get the right accounting advice, it was sloppily run and they employed too many people. They would point out it was the lack of snow in the Alps over the last few years that destroyed their business. But I think the company would still be around today if it had been run with more discipline.

When you're backing entrepreneurs, you've got to make sure they have a lot to lose – not only their jobs but also their homes or, at least, a substantial amount of money. These guys come to you claiming they know all about their products, all about marketing and all about financial discipline.

But in fact, you have to check on everything. If it's your money, you've got to be involved in the business yourself. Gradually the property market recovered, and we carried out a large scheme in Edinburgh which put us back on a solid footing. And when we floated the company in 1983, any other diversifications had to be sold, because the market wouldn't have understood.

I suppose it's in my blood to back small businesses, and we do have a number in our portfolio which are successful. But I'm a jolly sight more careful now.

17 November 1991

Chris Wright

Chris Wright, 47, is chairman of the Chrysalis Group, a world-wide music and media company with an annual turnover of about £100m. He formed Chrysalis Records in 1969 with Terry Ellis after leaving Manchester University. The company expanded into television production, juke boxes and fruit machines. In 1989, Wright sold 50 per cent of the Chrysalis records division to Thorn EMI for £40m. The remaining stake was sold to Thorn EMI last week. The organization has interests in TV, video production, recording studios, and music publishing, in addition to its record labels.

My biggest mistake was not moving to New York when my ex-partner returned to London in 1980.

Over the last few years, the newspapers have often written about the fact that Chrysalis has what is referred to as 'an American problem'. It's the biggest problem we've ever had.

Very few British companies have successfully invaded the US market-place; it's usually a graveyard. What can kill you is the scale of the infrastructure needed to operate in a market that big. You have to cover the whole country, and it's very expensive having offices in New York and Los Angeles.

When we started the company, I used to spend the bulk of my time out there. Then, for many years, my ex-partner, Terry Ellis, ran the US side from Los Angeles. The company's problems really started when he moved back. He attempted to run the US companies by commuting, which was very difficult. As a result of the company's problems and of working together in the same office, we ended up falling out and dissolving our partnership. I thought long and hard at that point about whether to move to New York and take control of what we were doing in the US. The British company was strong enough to withstand my absence.

But I had a pretty good lifestyle in England. I had a family here, my children were at various stages of their education, and I didn't want to uproot them. Unfortunately, it's no good just commuting; you have to be a presence in the marketplace.

In my view, companies are only capable of succeeding if the principal either spends an awful lot of time there, or, better still, goes there to live. Alternatively, you need to find an American executive who has the charisma to take over the personification of the company himself.

The record industry requires figureheads. You need to have somebody on both sides of the Atlantic.

If there's a president, the American artist wants to meet him. The Americans are very patriotic. They welcome you as a friend and a businessman if you live there. But if you're representing a foreign company you're regarded as a bit of a carpetbagger.

By trying to straddle both sides of the Atlantic, the company's efforts became dissipated. And the American company didn't get the benefit of my full-time presence.

I believe if I'd moved there when my ex-partner came back, and let him take over the British company, I would have been on top of the problems, and been able to provide creative direction. It would probably have preserved the partnership.

Having not done that, I should have immediately bitten the bullet and gone when he left in 1984.

Instead, I put my family in front of my business. As a result, Chrysalis in America continued to lose money throughout the 1980s until it became necessary to sell 50 per cent of the record business to EMI, which resulted in being my next biggest mistake.

In selling the first half of Chrysalis Records to EMI in 1989, I rather naively believed that the establishment of the resulting joint venture would eliminate all the financial problems within the record division. But we were unable to produce any cost savings. Furthermore, EMI could not achieve any savings because they could not absorb Chrysalis into any of their structures. The only solution was for EMI to acquire the remaining 50 per cent of Chrysalis Records.

24 November 1991

Gerry Cottle

Gerry Cottle, 46, is chairman of Gerry Cottle's Circus. He started it
in 1970 with two Shetland ponies, a tent and a lorry. With a partner,
he toured the villages of Devon and Cornwall, horse-riding, juggling
and stilt-walking. By 1974 he had two circuses and a staff of 60
touring Britain; by 1976 they were performing overseas. Despite
financial disaster in 1980 when the company went into liquidation,
he soon bounced back and today is more successful than ever.

My biggest mistake was taking my circus to Iran in 1978. It was a
complete disaster.

It wasn't our first taste of the Middle East. Two years earlier we had
been invited to perform for the Sultan of Oman's birthday celebrations
and also in Bahrain, and these had been very successful.

Then in 1978, we were invited to Sharjah for four weeks. Our two
circuses in England were permanently booked, so we had to set up a third
unit, which really overstretched the management.

It meant taking on another 50 people, including ringmasters, artists,
musicians, electricians and so on, and cost around £100,000, which was a
lot of money in those days.

At the time we thought it was worth it, because we had also been
invited to perform for the Shah of Iran. We were to open in Tehran, then
tour for six months, and they were going to pay us £10,000 a week.

We booked world-class acts at world-class prices. It took three months
to set everything up, but this was the job we had been waiting for. The
opening site was the Olympic sports stadium in Tehran, and they had
offered us accommodation in new blocks of apartments.

Everything went well in Sharjah, but the apartments in Iran had holes
in the ground for lavatories, and the food was served by people wearing
filthy rubber gloves. I went to Tehran to troubleshoot, and found our
chimpanzees had been kept in their travelling-boxes at the airport for two
weeks. I had to give a back-hander to the right people to get them out.

We were moved to hotels, which they said they would pay for, but
somehow the money never appeared. Meanwhile, the lions still had to be
fed, the staff had to be paid, and we kept needing spares sent over from
the UK because the new stadium was so badly equipped.

We were dealing with a man who was never available. Every time we went to see him we were given a different excuse and told to try again later. On top of it all, the circus had only been running for a couple of weeks when riots broke out. A curfew was imposed from 6pm, and our show didn't start until 8pm, so our audience consisted of government officials and their families, while the general public couldn't get in.

We were begging for money, and constantly setting up meetings with people who didn't turn up. For some reason, whenever we mentioned money, most of them lost their ability to speak English. The rest kept telling us not to panic, the money was on its way, 'God willing'.

He obviously wasn't, because the money never did arrive. Finally I told them we would have to return to the UK, and they responded with all sorts of threats.

We managed to get out, but the whole fiasco cost us around £250,000. We kept our word and paid everybody ourselves, but it milked our business in the UK.

As a result, we went into voluntary liquidation in February 1979. It was a dark and dismal period, and we lost a lot of credibility and confidence. We had to start all over again, renting other people's tents and animals. But then we had some phenomenally successful tours in the Far East which put us back on our feet.

Ever since, whenever we go abroad, we have always insisted on all costs being paid up front, so only profits are at risk. And while we continue to perform in the Middle East, I don't think we'll ever go back to Iran.

15 December 1991

Cees Zwaard

Cees Zwaard, 40, is the managing director of RCA Columbia Pictures Video UK. He was born in the Netherlands and took a business course at a college in The Hague, which was funded by multiple retailers. On completing the course, he entered the music industry. By 1981, he was sales and marketing manager of EMI Records Holland. He then moved into video as marketing manager of Thorn EMI, and in 1983 became managing director of RCA Columbia Pictures in Holland. Five years later, he arrived in London to take up his present position.

My biggest mistake was believing I could get other video distributors in Britain to work together towards a common goal.

When there is an industry problem in Holland, because it's such a small country all the different companies join forces. As a result, it's the eleventh economic power in the world.

In 1990, when the UK video market dropped drastically within the space of three months, I had an idea to combine all our advertising and promotional money into one big campaign in order to persuade the public that hiring a video is an entertaining way to spend an evening.

We did exactly the same thing in Holland and it boosted the market by 60 per cent. That campaign is now in its seventh year.

So I approached nine other managing directors through the British Videogram Association, and initially the response was very good.

The difficulties began when everyone had to agree on a creative concept after we appointed an advertising agency. The debate was over whether to show products or a habit.

We thought it was more important to get across the message that hiring a video was an alternative form of entertainment rather than show clips of what was available. I wanted people who actually rented videos to appear in the commercials.

But everybody had different ideas, and it took six months to come up with a compromise. In this country, people like talking, but they don't like making joint decisions.

The first commercial showed one wildebeest asking another where all the rest had gone, and he was told they were all at home watching a video. It was a good creative concept in itself, but it became a 60-second commercial broken up with three film clips, which made it very difficult to follow.

We argued and argued, though probably I should have pushed my point of view harder.

It was terribly frustrating; they had a very short-term approach and were more concerned about this month's sales.

The second commercial was completely product led, which was the complete opposite of what I wanted. Research has shown that using film clips is extremely confusing for consumers, because they don't know whether it's a satellite, cinema, TV or video advertisement.

We were very unhappy about it and said we didn't want to waste our time and money on something that didn't work. Being chairman of the committee had taken up about 20 per cent of my time over a period of eight months.

It was supposed to be a £10m campaign, with everybody contributing according to their market share. Our share was about 30 per cent, so when we pulled out there wasn't enough money left for them to continue.

Last November, we reworked our original concept and tested it in the Granada area. It had a more positive response from consumers and dealers. The commercial showed ordinary members of the public talking about video, which was exactly what I wanted to do 18 months ago, and the production costs were only 10 per cent of the previous one.

Because of its success, a lot of people have been asking if I will allow other distributors to come in with us again. The answer is simple. If they like what I am doing, they can send me a cheque, and I'll do the work. But I'm not making any changes to my commercial.

29 December 1991

Angus Rankine

Angus Rankine, 33, is managing director of Jacqueline de Baer, the corporate clothing design house. After four years with Barclays Bank on the graduate trainee scheme, he became an account director with J Walter Thompson in 1981. In his last twelve months with JWT he was seconded to the development team at Canary Wharf to act as marketing consultant, and consequently was asked to join Olympia & York in 1986 to set up and run the department. After five years he left to join Jacqueline de Baer, who recently won the TSB/Options 'Women Mean Business' award.

My biggest mistake was giving too large a contract to one supplier when I was running the marketing department at Canary Wharf.

In 1989 we had the largest architectural model-building programme in the world. We split the project into two. The base was to be made by a London company called Presentation Unit at a cost of £350,000.

The contract for the buildings, worth $850,000 (£470,000) went to Dimensional Presentations in Los Angeles, which was the largest model maker in the world, and appeared at the time to be the most competent. We paid a third up-front to cover materials and advance labour, which is standard practice, and within three months, through financial mismanagement, Dimensional Presentations went into Chapter 11 bankruptcy.

I had to go out there to assess the circumstances, and I took our London-based model maker with me. The bailiffs were due in at 10am on the Monday, which meant they could take all the work in progress and seal it for up to three months. I was faced with a number of alternatives. I could get a new model maker to start from scratch, recommend to Olympia & York that it purchase Dimensional Presentations, allow someone else to buy the company and lose any control I might have had, or watch over while our London-based model maker bought it.

We opted for the last, and the model maker would probably describe this as his biggest mistake. He had just 48 hours to put together a package and buy the firm, which he managed to do on the Sunday night.

We were then presented with a pile of Perspex, glue and paint without any instructions. It was not dissimilar to trying to put together an Airfix kit as a model you have never seen before.

The majority of the Perspex had been cut. All the pieces were there, but trying to work out which pile related to which building, which colour paints were meant to be applied, and so on, seemed impossible.

We had three weeks in which to do it, so we just had to roll up our sleeves and get on with it.

I remember standing on the shop floor at midnight, staring at these piles of Perspex, saying to myself: 'What have we done?'

It really was a hellish experience. Because it happened over the Christmas period while everyone else was off, nobody ever understood what an incredible amount of hard work we had put in.

In the end, the model was delivered for only 10 per cent more than it should have cost, albeit some two months late. But I learnt a lot from that mistake. Firstly, I shouldn't have put so such work with one model maker. There are perhaps 30 top-quality model-making firms in the world, of which only 10 possess the computer equipment necessary for such a sophisticated project.

Out of those, only one or two could have handled a contract of that size, so the flexibility was absolutely minimal.

But we should have had greater control over how they spent the deposit. We should have established a system so that we knew what they were doing week by week instead of trusting to their reputation and long-distance promises. I will never again put so many eggs into one basket. In fact, I don't think you should put more than 40 per cent of your business into any one firm. You should also make sure that your order does not represent more than 40 per cent of your supplier's business.

2 February 1992

Malcolm Hurlston

> Malcolm Hurlston, 53, is an independent corporate consultant specializing in consumer credit and public affairs. He is chairman of the Government-owned Student Loans Company, of the Esop Centre, which promotes employee share ownership, and of Euroshop, an organization of retailer and consumer groups, and of Registry Trust, which operates the registry of county court judgements. He played a leading role in establishing Unity Trust Bank, the trade union financial institution, and is an adviser to numerous organizations, including B&Q and the Co-operative Bank.

My biggest mistake was to be so carried away by a fine turn of phrase from a politician that I made a decision I came to regret.

It was in 1971, when John Davies was Secretary of State for Trade and Industry. The economy needed shaking out and the question arose of what the Government should do about it: come to the rescue of firms in trouble – which had been the tendency – or allow them to go under?

John Davies made a key speech in which he said the Government would not rescue any lame ducks, and this heralded a whole new tough approach. At the time, I was an adviser to the British Insurance Association. During the 1960s one or two insurance companies had come into the market who were not members. They offered cheaper policies and took away quite a lot of market share from the traditional companies.

When they went bust nobody was surprised, although the BIA stressed the value of insuring with members.

Then one of the member companies – Vehicle and General – went bust. By that stage it had acquired several hundred thousand policy-holders, and it was therefore a pretty serious matter.

The members of the BIA came together to decide what to do, and pulled in a firm of accountants to have a look.

I was looking at this problem from the point of view of how the industry ought to behave. There were several factors to consider, such as whether long-term confidence in motor insurance would be affected by a major company going bust, and whether there was a moral obligation on the BIA after recommending that motorists go to members.

The sum involved, although it now seems quite small, was of the order of £20m. It was the first and last crash on that scale in the business, and it was the companies that had lost customers to Vehicle and General that were being asked to pick up the tab, which was clearly unfair.

My view was that in the light of what John Davies had said about lame ducks, it was wise to let Vehicle and General go to the wall and not rescue it. It would be a salutary lesson for people, showing them it was not sensible to choose an insurer on price alone.

When Vehicle and General went down, the outstanding claims – other than those which were picked up by the industry agreement for serious cases – were not settled.

In time, I began to feel that public confidence in insurance had ebbed as a result of us failing to come to the rescue.

Had the decision gone the other way, those people who had put in claims would have got their money and there would have been less government intervention.

It was a mistake to be too influenced by the short-term political climate. In the end, when things did go badly, the government nearly always bowed to pressure to do something about it.

The exigencies of politics call for short-term statements and decisions, as Harold Wilson pointed out when he talked about a week being a long time in politics.

But businesses do not generally work to electoral cycles, nor do the long-term relationships between people and the goods and services they buy. Ever since then, I have always tried to take a longer-term view when making a decision. And I have learned to be suspicious whenever I come across a statement that smacks of phrase-making – a statement in which the words themselves are quite exciting.

9 February 1992

Caroline Charles

Caroline Charles, 49, started the Caroline Charles design company in 1963, and made her name designing clothes for such celebrities as Mick Jagger, Ringo Starr, Barbra Streisand and Lulu. Within two years she had tied up with an American fashion group, but the deal fell apart, forcing her to start again. Her first retail outlet opened in 1977 in London's Beauchamp Place, and by the 1980s Caroline Charles had an extensive licensing programme in Japan. Today she exports all over the world, with designs ranging from accessories to bedlinens.

My biggest mistake was agreeing to sell out to the American group without protecting my own interests.

The Swinging Sixties were very heady times. The French, the Italians and the Americans came to London in droves to buy British fashion. It was easy, if you had something to offer, to do a great deal of business.

We were supplying various chains of stores in America, and one of them was owned by Jonathan Logan, which at the time was the largest garment business in the world.

There was something different about our approach, and the president of the group liked our quirkiness. He made us an offer and began to do things like flying us over for the day, which we found both amusing and flattering. We knew we were good at designing and promotion, but we had to start making clothes in quantity and sort out distribution, and that needed funding. The biggest in the world is somehow very beguiling, and I thought, 'Heavens, this must be the way to go.' They were buying what was currently the talk of the town – a young British designer connected with the Beatles, with garments they could make and sell in quantity.

We were accustomed to negotiating with factories on the outskirts of London, which was all we could afford, but tying up with Jonathan Logan meant the use of 42 factories in America and a showroom on Broadway.

We negotiated very quickly, and everything seemed to be fine. I was constantly travelling to and from the States, and everybody's wages were being paid by Jonathan Logan.

I was kept being told that the new company was in the process of being formed and that I was on the board. I wasn't to worry about anything, these lawyers just take a bit of time.

The garments were manufactured and distributed, and they put money behind an advertising campaign.

Six months down the line I was on a promotional tour of 23 American cities in something like three weeks when they suddenly called a halt.

They said they would only go ahead if I shut down the operation in Britain, moved to America and did it all from there.

I was terribly shocked, and said no.

So I came back to the UK, determined to get the show on the road again, but this time I was a lot more suspicious. I made sure we built the business up ourselves so we could not fall into the same trap.

It was a difficult time because they had the use of my name. The company was folded and I had to start again as Carmal Enterprises, though finally I got the name Caroline Charles back.

On the surface, tying up with the Americans had seemed a golden opportunity. It wasn't a mistake to think it would work out; the mistake was not to safeguard my company just in case it didn't.

I should have got involved with the planning and made them commit themselves to what they were going to do with the company once the purchase was completed. And I should have made sure that if it all went wrong, I wouldn't have to start all over again.

For someone of 22 it is very nice to have America on your doorstep, but the biggest is not necessarily the best when it comes to nourishing a small company, and it was a mistake to leap too fast.

Financially, we came out of it with no flags flying at all, but it was a great experience and I don't regret it. It was just a shame it didn't work out.

16 February 1992

Brendan Bruce

Brendan Bruce, 40, was appointed by Margaret Thatcher as the Conservative Party's director of communications in the spring of 1989 and was one of her principal image-makers. His career began in advertising after he took a degree in history and politics at Warwick University. In 1979 he became a director of Fletcher Shelton Delaney, in 1983 a director of Ted Bates, and in 1985 a director of D M B & B. In 1988 he ran Lord Young's DTI campaign to popularize the single European market. His book, *Images of Power*, is published by Kogan Page.

My biggest mistake was to present Mrs Thatcher as something she wasn't. In the summer of 1989, when she was approaching her 64th birthday, I planned to film her in a party political broadcast.

Although no one in the media had expressed any deep concern about her age, as they had with Ronald Reagan, I was keen that they shouldn't start. So the objective of the broadcast was to present her in the most youthful way we could, whilst maintaining her prime ministerial persona.

With a combination of make-up, lighting and lenses you can make anybody look like anything you want, but it's more difficult to do it on video. So I got Terence Donovan to shoot on 35mm film and Barbara Daley to do the make-up. You can't use Number 10 for party purposes because it's a government building, so we borrowed the drawing-room of a rather grand flat in Warwick Square.

The filming itself was perfectly routine. The Prime Minister was extremely experienced at reading an autocue and virtually directed herself. On the ninth take she pronounced herself satisfied.

I saw the film the following day, and the careful use of make-up, lighting and lenses had indeed taken about ten years off her age. But combined with the drawing-room setting, the effect went beyond being prime ministerial. In fact, it was quasi-regal.

I was bearing in mind a report which had shown that how we look and behave accounts for 55 per cent of the impact we make. How we speak accounts for another 38 per cent but what we're actually saying accounts for only 7 per cent.

It started to nag at me that we had gone too far by presenting Mrs Thatcher in this way, so I commissioned some research, and this is where I discovered the mistake.

People were used to seeing Mrs T being interviewed on video – without all the lighting and lenses and make-up – so the whole look of what we had done appeared artificial to them. Moreover, it made them start to question what she was saying, because one artificiality damages credibility.

In addition, Mrs T has a vivid personality which viewers usually experienced when interviewers said, 'Well, it's a horrible mess, and it's all your fault,' whereupon she would dispose of them in vivid and energetic language. But in this case she was reading from an autocue, and it came across to the viewer as formal and stilted.

A lot of image-makers get very worried about their principal's weaknesses. Instead of identifying the strengths and building on those, they start trying to make up for the weaknesses.

There is therefore a tendency to present leaders in a way that is not natural. And the public, when they know that person well, will always spot it. No one gets to the top without having fundamental strengths, and they're what you must concentrate on. Never put them in an artificial environment; never ask them to do something that they wouldn't do naturally, and always remember that perception is the only reality.

We undermined her credibility by presenting her in a way that looked artificial, and increased a feeling of distance from the voter with this grand, almost regal setting.

There wasn't time to film it again because it was due to be broadcast the next day. Luckily, because she had such a strong image, a one-off political broadcast like this could not undermine it. But I learned a lot from that mistake and made sure there was no repetition.

15 March 1992

Dan Wagner

Dan Wagner, 28, is managing director of MAID (Market Analysis and Information Database), which claims to be the world's biggest on-line marketing intelligence and data retrieval service. He founded the company in 1985, when he was 21 and a junior account executive with WCRS, the advertising agency. The idea came to him because he was irritated by the time spent in the agency's library digging out research reports. He decided to create an electronic database giving instant access on a company PC to marketing information from publications all over the world.

I reckon I made more than one big mistake since I set up MAID, but my biggest was launching it in the UK rather than in the United States. For I grossly underestimated the reluctance of UK marketing and advertising executives to take on something new – especially something that involved using computers. It nearly sunk MAID.

My initial research had revealed that there were some 300 on-line databases in the world but none serving the advertising and marketing industry. I had also counted up how many computers were in use at potential clients in the UK. But I failed to check who used them. It didn't take long to discover it wasn't the advertising and marketing people but the accountants.

I knew that a computerized library of marketing information was so much more efficient than information on index cards and masses of paper files. I felt sure that, once they saw our package, people would be queueing up to buy it – for we had concluded exclusive deals with the Economist Intelligence Unit, Euromonitor, Mintel and other information publishers to put their marketing reports on our mainframe.

But I was sorely mistaken.

There was still an extraordinary ignorance (or fear?) of computers among UK business executives in 1985.

I was astonished at the reluctance of marketing men to see me, or to attend a demonstration. Even when they did agree to view the package, I found an unexpected resistance to take on something that was new to them. Our target was to make four sales a month. In fact, we made one solitary sale in the first three months and no more than a miserable three in the first six months.

We were losing money at a frightening rate. Then in May 1986, I learned that an information trade show was to be held in New York. I decided to head there. That decision was a turning point.

Within five days of landing at Kennedy Airport, I signed up five blue-chip subscribers, including Colgate-Palmolive, Citibank and BBD&O, the largest ad agency in the world. I was over the moon.

Computers were far more widely used by business management in the US. Marketing executives quickly latched on to the value of an on-line database. Once they saw our system demonstrated, the immediate response was: 'OK, I'll buy it.'

I flew back to London elated. And after telling my tale to my sales director, Tony Sharp, we decided to return that same night to New York. Working from our hotel room by telephone, we managed to set up six demonstrations a day. The Americans were not in the least put off by our youthful enthusiasm. In six weeks of hard selling, we had a bagful of big names such as Coca-Cola and Ford. Twenty of the 30 biggest ad agencies in the US are now subscribers and we have a permanent office in New York headed by Tony Sharp.

Our success in the States gave us the boost we needed and before long we were signing up blue-chip names in the UK and elsewhere. We now have more than 3,000 subscribers world-wide, with most of them in the UK, including Asda, Boots, British Telecom, Cadbury-Schweppes, the DTI and Saatchi & Saatchi.

We're now one of the few information retrieval systems actually making money. In fact, despite the recession, 1991 was our best year so far. But financial success would have come to us a lot sooner if we had launched in the US in the first place.

22 March 1992

Roger Parry

Roger Parry, 38, is development director of Aegis, the financial holding company which owns Cavat, the leading media planning and buying specialist in Europe. He was educated at Bristol and Oxford universities, and from 1977 was a television and radio reporter and producer for the BBC, IRN, and Radio 4's Today programme, among others. In 1985, he joined McKinsey and Co, the consulting firm, working mostly overseas before joining Aegis three years later. His book, *People Businesses: Making Professional Firms Profitable*, is published by Century Business.

My big mistake was in believing that an idea which made overwhelming commercial sense would be readily accepted by a national industry. I did not realize the importance of politics and vested interests.

In 1983 I became programme director of a new company, Network Radio Productions, which had been formed to provide syndicated radio shows to the then struggling stations of the independent Radio Network. This was novel in the UK, although well established in the United States. Our aim was to revolutionize the industry.

In the early 1980s, independent radio stations were in trouble. Created by the Government as a response to the seaborne pirate radio ships, they were locally focused, fiercely independent units, intended to expand audience choice. The big, city-based stations were reasonably profitable, but the majority had failed to attract significant advertising revenue and were competing hard for audiences against the BBC local network.

British commercial radio was artistically mediocre and a commercial failure. The stations failed to co-operate to keep costs down, and failed to sell themselves as a network to national advertisers. Low revenues put pressure on programme budgets which led to an endless round of phone-ins and music shows.

Convinced that we were on to a winner, the NRP team started trying to sell the plan to the industry. It would only work if the majority of stations, including the big ones, could see beyond their narrow interests. True, we would have made money as the programme syndicator, but they would have made much more as audiences and revenues boomed.

We developed a chat show using national personalities, who in many cases would have been too expensive for local radio but were happy to do a networked show.

We created a soap opera, a weekly comedy revue, devised a network top-10 chart show with a potential sponsor all lined up, and so on. Our package of six programmes was greeted with enthusiasm by the small stations; with paternalistic, if bemused, approval by the IBA; with caution but acceptance by the industry's trade association; and with polite interest by the big, city-based stations, most of which then worked behind the scenes to make sure it never happened.

'Why let outsiders into the magic circle,' some of them argued, 'when we can do the whole thing ourselves and keep the profits?'

Looking back, it was naive in the extreme for us to think that a small number of big companies would risk their narrow commercial interests to benefit others.

To us, as outsiders, it was obvious that without syndicated programmes to support them, the smaller stations would fail and be taken over by their larger cousins. The whole idea of a network of autonomous local broadcasters needs network programmes. The lesson is, if you want to change an industry for the better, simply demonstrating the economic potential is not enough. The powerful must be won over, or at least persuaded to be neutral. Those with a vested interest to see the change succeed must be organized, public opinion mobilized, and potential opponents must not be alerted until the idea is a *fait accompli*.

If all of that sounds more like playing politics than doing business, I feel that I learned that is exactly what organizing a minor industrial revolution is all about.

10 May 1992

Julia Cleverdon

Julia Cleverdon, 42, is chief executive of Business in the Community which in July celebrates ten years of activity. She began her career with British Leyland in 1972 after reading history at Cambridge. The following year she joined the Industrial Society, then in 1974 became a consultant to Anglo-American Mining Corporation in South Africa. Returning to the Industrial Society in 1975, she ran several campaigns and established its education and inner-city division. In 1988 she joined Business in the Community and rose to become joint managing director and then chief executive.

My biggest mistake was trying to keep too many plates spinning at once. I discovered my passion for campaigns while at Cambridge. From compulsory bicycle classes for freshers, to security improvements, I could always think of things that ought to be done.

When I worked for British Leyland, I was forever running campaigns to improve communications and get employees more involved.

Then I joined the Industrial Society, where in 1978 I was in charge of a campaign to explain to everybody in different parts of society the importance of industry.

I poured out ideas all over the organization as to what we could do. We needed to write pamphlets for the Women's Institute, explaining why industry matters; produce books for six-year-olds about a visit to a factory; set up student industrial societies; get Marks & Spencer to put leaflets in their carrier bags . . .

I soon found myself racing about, from making speeches to the WI to launching books in primary schools, to talking to student industrial societies.

As time went by, it became increasingly unclear to me as to what the priorities were, and the same for the team around me.

But I didn't actually realize this until the night we had a satellite link for a debate between the Oxford and Cambridge unions. The subject was: 'This house believes there is no time more worthy than that spent in industry.' It suddenly dawned on me that we hadn't done the necessary preparation to get that debate properly run. We hadn't got good enough arguments, and we were in danger of losing.

What I learned, as it became more and more difficult to manage those ideas and see them through to the end, is that you have to pay very close attention to how many plates you can actually spin.

Personally I don't believe you can manage more than three. You can still have masses of ideas, but you need other people to take them up. The crunch came with the annual general meeting of the WI at the Albert Hall, when women gather from all over Britain to vote on the various resolutions which have been put forward over the year.

We had managed to get onto the agenda: 'We in the WI commit ourselves to encouraging greater understanding of the importance of industry.' But instead of backing the motion, delegation after delegation stood up and attacked it on the grounds that industry was responsible for pollution – for killing fish, for soot on your sheets, and so on. Not for creating wealth, providing jobs, producing services.

In spite of what I thought was a lot of work and a lot of support to the WI, the resolution failed. In horror, I realized that everything we had worked for in the previous two years of the campaign had come to nothing. It was the worst moment of my life.

By failing to concentrate my time and energy, I had allowed a crucial plate to spin off. I never made that mistake again. These days, I pick my three key targets and make sure that I have someone to discuss them with on a regular basis.

This is why I believe that the roles of chairman and chief executive should be filled by different people: it gives the chief executive the opportunity to talk everything through.

It doesn't particularly mean the chairman is going to change anything, but the very act of saying, 'This is what I'm tilting at,' helps you to focus on your objectives.'

7 June 1992

Roger Saul

Roger Saul, 40, founded Mulberry with £500 at the age of 21 in his parent's garage in Chilcompton, Somerset. While a business studies student, he started designing leather accessories, and the company quickly expanded to the design and manufacture of English country-style leather goods and clothing. His father and his wife both work at Mulberry. In the 1980s a chain of shops was added which now produces a turnover of £30m. About 80 per cent of output is exported.

My biggest mistake was to fall for the American Dream. I started Mulberry in 1971 as a business student with £500 and a strong desire to succeed as a designer, primarily of accessories. It was an exciting time for fashion and we were successful from the start. But the better end of the British fashion market was tiny compared to continental Europe so we started exporting to Italy and France.

By 1974 we were also exporting beyond Europe, including to the US, Japan and Australia. We rocketed through the 1970s, adding handbags and then clothing, and building up our own manufacturing operation. By 1979 we were turning over £1.25m and won a Queen's Award for Export.

At the time about 30 per cent of our production was destined for the US. We had one of the best accessory brands in America and sold to all the leading department stores and shops. But the fashion market in the US is very volatile, much more so than in Europe. The buyers are always changing their jobs and the designers they buy from.

I had believed that by 'going domestic' we would tap into the bigger buying budgets. US buyers gave most of their business to the producers with a base in the US and although they were beginning to buy more from European companies I wanted Mulberry to become domestically available. So we opened an office and a showroom in New York.

But then the recession hit harder than expected, and the difference between the dollar and sterling meant a 50 per cent rise in the retail prices of our products.

The net effect was that just as we were receiving our Queen's Award our US business for the next season was disappearing. Looking back at that time is like looking into a black hole. It was immensely depressing. We had never seen anything like it before and could not see what to do next.

Fortunately, the European and Japanese markets were reasonably buoyant, providing some support. But our turnover fell from £1.25m to £700,000 over about six months. We had to make people redundant and cut overheads drastically. It was a very hard, sobering lesson. But it was a good one, too. We learnt about the rough side of cash flow. We realized that the only way we could continue to reach customers, build the brand and keep up sales as the recession hit Europe was to go into retailing ourselves.

In 1980–1, as others cut back or went to the wall, we opened shops, initially in Paris, then the fashion capital of the world, and London. It was a risk, but I really felt we had no choice. There was no other way to control our destiny and succeed world-wide. Businesses such as Giorgio Armani, Kenzo, Ralph Lauren took the same decision. Happily it paid off. My mistake had been to invest too much in the US market and to believe in the American Dream. But it was like a volatile love affair, it simply could not last.

Now we have 35 shops world-wide which provide the shop window for a thriving international wholesale business. I have only returned to the US once in the last seven years and we will only return there with our own shops rather than as a wholesaler. We view America with as much trepidation as ever, particularly as it heads into the next recession. To date, we have concentrated on positioning Mulberry as a high quality, original and quintessentially English brand in Europe, the Far East and Japan.

21 October 1990

Lord Rees-Mogg

LORD Rees-Mogg, 60, is a businessman, author, columnist, book dealer and television censor. He is chairman of his own rare book shop, Pickering and Chatto, and a director of GEC. He was a journalist on the *Financial Times* and *Sunday Times*. When editor of *The Times* from 1967 to 1981, he was also on the executive board of Times Newspapers. In the 1980s, he was chairman of the Arts Council, where he presided over a policy of regional development, and a deputy chairman of the BBC.

The greatest mistake I ever made was agreeing to the shutdown of *The Times* in 1978 without having a Wapping-style solution in sight. At the time, the Times Newspapers group, owned by the International Thomson Organization, was riven with union problems.

We had 64 different union chapels within the group. Any one of them was capable of stopping the newspapers and they were doing so only too often. We had been engaged for a considerable time in fruitless negotiations on changing working practices with the unions. In one case we had been in discussions with the unions since the middle 1960s.

The changeover from the old-fashioned hot metal process for producing newspapers to the new technology had already taken place in other countries and forcing the issue seemed, in terms of business ethics, to be thoroughly justified. But we reckoned without the dissension within the unions. We also had no let out in case the strategy failed.

The Thomson head board, which I was not on, wanted to face up to the unions. The decision to force the issue was the result of quite careful planning. We had a meeting with the unions in February of 1978 and as a result of that meeting the decision was taken to shut down the papers in November. The Thomson board thought this would lead to the unions accepting new technology, and indeed, this was what the union general secretaries had told us. 'I cannot give you what you want unless you point a pistol at my head,' one of the general secretaries said to us.

The basic strategy failure, which is clear in retrospect, was that we should never have gone into the confrontation on the basis of a bluff. Insanely, I failed to see that the logic required we had an alternative in case the strategy failed.

We also placed much too much faith in the union bosses. However, the militants in the print unions were only too happy to embarrass the union general secretaries and the general secretaries were in fact extremely feeble. They made public statements supporting the militants, while criticizing them privately to us.

I had always favoured a Wapping-style solution, setting up a new printing plant on a greenfield site, and I tried to create an alternative during the dispute by taking *The Times* to Frankfurt. It seemed to me a move in the right direction and we did print one copy in Frankfurt. I have a copy of it framed at home. But the Frankfurt option did not have the backing of the Thomson board.

They were frightened of the consequences and we had to abandon it. The British unions won support from the West German unions and the police in Frankfurt became very worried about the risk of violent protests. There was in fact a shot fired at the head of the printing plant we had used in Frankfurt.

The shutdown of the Times Newspapers, which lasted for nearly a year, cost about £40m in 1980 money and the person it benefited in the end was, ironically, Rupert Murdoch. The strike precipitated the decision to sell the papers and the feeling in the Thomson Organisation was that Rupert Murdoch was the only proprietor around who was tough enough to do what we had failed to do. We had played into the union militants' hands. But they in turn played into Mr Murdoch's.

When Wapping happened, Mr Murdoch knew exactly what he was going to do if the unions did not agree to what he wanted. In fact, he did not want them to agree to his conditions.

I cannot think looking back on it how I came to agree to the shutdown policy without having an alternative strategy in place. But I have not had occasion to make the same mistake again. It was rather special circumstances.

11 March 1990

Debbie Moore

Former leading model Debbie Moore started a business running dance studios in 1979 and took Pineapple Group public in 1982. In March 1988 she bought out the original dance and fashion part of the business. The remaining public company was bought by Doctus, a marketing and management consultancy, for £44m last year. Pineapple Limited, the private company, has a turnover of £3m and expects to make a profit of £200,000 this year.

In business you make many mistakes and in retrospect one of my biggest – which was a recurring one – was not to stick to my convictions when I knew instinctively something was wrong. As I say in my book *When a Woman Means Business*, one of the golden rules is 'don't rely on the experts'.

When I was chairman of Pineapple Group plc, alongside the dance studios and fitness business, we were a rapidly expanding fashion business and needed to computerize our systems. I am not very computer literate and had only ever used the basics.

We were approached by a company which came recommended. They told us they were offering us a package which they had installed for Speedo, a clothing and swimwear company. The main things that the system was supposed to do were to keep control of the stock, to monitor sales by style and colour and do invoicing. They said Speedo were satisfied with the system and, although their business was slightly simpler then ours, we decided to go ahead. I wanted to keep the manual systems as back-up. The accountancy advisers just let them go because they thought the new computerized systems would be implemented fairly quickly. They told me that this was therefore unnecessary. I was lulled into a false sense of security and didn't insist.

The consultant, a 'computer genius', was set up in an open plan office at our warehouse on the Holloway Road, north London. I knew something was wrong because the consultant, who was costing us a vast amount of money, was always on the phone to the software company, and there was no information coming through. We didn't have stock analysis or sales figures and time was going by – and we had lost our manual system. Also, people started calling up saying that they had received the wrong order or that the invoices were incorrect, which of course meant delays in payments. The consultant was clearly having problems – he seemed to be smoking more and more. (Wherever he was standing he was always surrounded by at least 30 cigarette ends.)

At this point I insisted that the computer must be faulty. The computer expert and all the accountants and the financial people – which you get when you're a plc and shed when you go private – thought this was a hilarious statement. They were astonished that, after three months of work, I even dared to say it. What did I know about computers, they asked. Consequently, at the time I thought it wasn't the right thing to have said and I left the expert to get on with it again.

We had the computer for the best part of nine months and it never worked properly. We only found out there really was a problem when the consultant left the computer company. Then he came to us to say that he could help with all the things that had gone wrong. This was the first time that anyone admitted that the package we had was not the same as the one which had been in use at Speedo, but a modified version (which had never worked before or since).

In the end the whole operation cost about £100,000 for the hardware, software and the cost of the consultant (not to mention the time involved), which contributed to our losses that year.

It was a fairly crucial mistake, but a difficult one to avoid as we had done everything by the book and seen the system in operation. How were we to know they would put in a different system? As soon as I was suspicious I should have implemented the manual system again and insisted that someone else come in to have a look at the computer.

Common sense should prevail in a business and you must always be insistent and not be undermined by the 'experts'.

4 March 1990

George Bull

After his first year in the drinks business, George Bull celebrated his employer's sales reaching £1m. Thirty years later he is chairman of its successor, International Distillers and Vintners, one of the world's three biggest liquor companies. Now he can celebrate sales of more than £2.5bn, profits of £400m and brands ranging from J & B and Smirnoff to IDV's own inventions: Croft Original sherry, Bailey's Irish Cream, Malibu and Aqua Libra.

I can distinctly recall not one but two major mistakes, both dating back a few years. One came when IDV was first taken over by Grand Metropolitan. I got permission to try to promote J & B within the group. I spent half an afternoon telling hundreds of executives from Watney's, Trumans, Mecca and Peter Dominic what a magnificent whisky it was.

The occasion was a bit spoilt when our chairman, the late Maxwell Joseph, muttered that he was sure Ski yoghurt, another Grand Met product, was going to make just as much, if not more, money than J & B.

Nevertheless, my persuasion worked and J & B promptly appeared in optics all over Britain. But then foreigners, used to the idea of J & B as a luxury premium brand, discovered it was just a commodity Scotch in its native Britain and the discovery was beginning to hurt sales in the rest of the world. So, a few years later I had the embarrassing job of telling my in-house customers that they would have to discourage buyers by upping the price and transforming it into the same premium brand as it was everywhere else in the world.

People outside the drinks business may not appreciate what a serious mistake it was because I'd jeopardized J & B's image, and that's the only asset any drinks brand has – apart from its intrinsic quality – and even a whisky as good as J & B can be hurt if it becomes associated with cheapness.

My other mistake was also a result of my own cockiness. We'd launched Croft Original sherry, one of the first really successful 'marketing' brands in the drinks business – in fact it was the first sherry sold under the Croft name, previously it had only been selling port. Then we tried to copy our success in the table wine market. We'd done a bit of market research and found that people liked the idea of drinking red wines, but thought that the ones actually on the market were too sharp, too hard, too tannic. Why not, we thought, devise a soft, smooth red wine?

So we took some rather ordinary Portuguese red – it was from Estremadura, I remember the whole disaster vividly – and sweetened it. The rules were rather less restrictive in those days. Then we took a rather dumpy bottle from a bottle bank and we were on our way. Or rather we weren't. Even the name – Doçura, reminding people of douce, softness – didn't help. We learnt a severe lesson: that people wouldn't touch something that wasn't really very good, even if it was heavily promoted.

Both stories have happy endings. J & B is still not a big seller here, though an awful lot of people are prepared to pay a premium price for it, but it's the second biggest-selling Scotch in the world, and its sales outside the United States have gone up eight times in the last fifteen years to more than four million cases. And that's not bad for a Scotch which was virtually unknown until the 1950s, and which depended on the US for 90 per cent of its sales until the 1960s.

And a few years after the Doçura disaster we applied the lesson we had learnt when we launched Piat d'Or. Like Doçura, this was soft and sweet, but it was a much better wine, based firmly on the wines we could buy from decent wine-growing areas in France and blended by people who applied the quality standards they had learnt from decades of drinking good claret. It now sells 2.5m cases world-wide and is France's largest exported table-wine brand. But that's another story.

25 February 1990

Sir Peter Thompson

Sir Peter Thompson has been successively chief executive and chairman of National Freight Corporation, now called NFC, since 1977 – three years before it was privatized in what has become a model employee buyout. A 61-year-old Yorkshireman, he read economics at Leeds University. He then joined Unilever, moving to GKN ten years later. In 1964, he was made transport controller of Rank Organisation, moving to British Steel three years later. He later became group co-ordinator of British Road Services, part of NFC. The success of NFC has made him an evangelist of the virtues of employee share ownership. The group was floated on the stock market in February 1989.

This is a cheat. I am about to describe what could have been my biggest mistake – which thanks to the wisdom of our non-executive directors, I was not allowed to make.

The time was 1980. The Thatcher government had just been elected and part of its manifesto included a commitment to privatize the National Freight Corporation. Norman Fowler, the shadow Transport Minister, who had written the paragraphs about NFC when in opposition, recognized that perhaps NFC as a whole would not be viable while it had to bear massive operating losses in the National Carriers Division.

National Carriers had included the cartage and sundries operations of British Rail and had been made part of NFC when it was set up by the then Labour government in 1968. In its first year of operation within NFC it had the distinction of losing £26m on a £26m turnover.

After much sweat and management attention, it was still making sizeable operating losses in 1980. In the election manifesto, Mr Fowler had offered as a possible solution that National Carriers should be taken out of NFC and given back to British Rail. There was a fierce debate at our board on whether we should take up the offer of returning it to BR or try to privatize NFC as a whole.

As chief executive, I wanted it out of NFC. All I could see ahead was the continuing grind of trying to make this business profitable. This would require many more redundancies, many depot closures, great cash outflows and, at the end of it all, there was no guarantee we would have a profitable business. I had no doubts. Send it back to British Rail with our best wishes.

The board was mainly non-executive. They argued that if we were not prepared to privatize NFC as a whole, maybe the government would take the view that we should sell off the profitable parts and leave us to manage the rump. Also, by returning an unprofitable non-transport business to the management of British Rail we could be spawning a subsidized competitor which would have the effect of depressing rates in the whole road transport market.

I was obdurate. They were adamant and they (the non-executives) outnumbered me. The decision was taken to advise secretary of state Mr Fowler that we wished to privatize NFC as a whole.

How wrong I was and how right they were. But perhaps not for the reasons that were at the centre of their argument. In 1980 no one envisaged how valuable the antiquated goods yards that were the operating base of National Carriers would prove to be. Today, we have solved the repositioning and profitability problems of National Carriers, but NFC still has in the property locker development sites such as the 20 acres behind Kings Cross, the eleven acres adjacent to Camden Lock and the 40 per cent interest in eleven acres adjacent to Paddington Station.

These are only the property jewels in the London area. There are many similar sites which we have already developed or will be developing in the provinces.

Thank God I was not allowed to make my mistake. *Vivent* non-executive directors!

18 February 1990

Sir Gordon Borrie

SIR Gordon Borrie has been Director General of Fair Trading for fourteen years. Appointed in 1976, he was reappointed for five-year terms in 1981 and 1986. Before moving to the Office of Fair Trading he was a barrister and professor of English law at Birmingham University.

My greatest mistake lay in being reluctant to promote a deal with the Stock Exchange on abolishing the market's restrictive practices. I insisted on pursuing the matter through the courts.

It sprang from the fact that in 1976 – by coincidence the year that I was appointed to my present job – the law on restrictive cartel arrangements was extended to cover services, including financial services. Previously, it had been confined to trade in goods.

As a result, many agreements were registered covering the supply of services offered by groups as varied as estate agents, the travel trade and actuaries.

My job is to scrutinize all cartel arrangements, and if they are significant and the offending parties will not abandon them, I must take their agreements before the Restrictive Practices Court.

Most of those covered by the extension of the law soon realized it was possible to modify their practices and satisfy the law, and that court proceedings were not inevitable, largely because I enjoy a statutory discretion not to go to court – provided the Secretary of State agrees. However compromise with the Stock Exchange seemed impossible. I was particularly concerned about the way members had to charge fixed minimum commissions, the 'single capacity' rule that prevented brokers and jobbers from doing each other's jobs, and the severe restrictions on shareholdings in member companies.

But the Stock Exchange was adamant that it was prepared to go to court and defend the rules to the death. So the Office of Fair Trading started court proceedings in 1979. They went on for four years.

Within weeks of the 1983 general election, Cecil Parkinson, the new Secretary of State for Trade and Industry, made a deal. In return for the Stock Exchange giving up minimum commissions, he would introduce legislation to stop the legal action.

We all knew minimum commissions were the basic foundation stone of the edifice of restrictive practices as a whole, so their abolition meant that 'Big Bang' was soon on the horizon.

My big mistake was to have played it by the book. With hindsight, it is doubtful that my court action could have achieved the desired results any sooner. Indeed, the chances are that lengthy court proceedings followed by an appeal would have delayed changes for a long time.

So Mr Parkinson was right. I had never sought to promote or encourage the sort of deal that he made in 1983. Indeed I expressed concern to him about what he was doing. I wanted the conventional outcome envisaged by the legislation, but Mr Parkinson's deal got rid of the restrictions more simply, quickly and cheaply.

Of course, I could not have made any sort of deal with the Stock Exchange myself. My duty to go to court remained until it was removed by an Act of Parliament in 1984. But a number of Mr Parkinson's predecessors had considered the possibility of stopping the case. I persuaded them that I, an independent statutory official, should be allowed to get on with what Parliament required me to do.

I could have put an end to the Stock Exchange's restrictions not only earlier than through court proceedings, but even earlier than Mr Parkinson did if I had urged his predecessors to look for a non-judicial way out. London as a centre for international investment transactions might have been deregulated that much sooner. That, I believe, would have been beneficial. This lawyer has learned from the episode to look not only at the law but also round it for alternative solutions.

11 February 1990

Gerald Ratner

Gerald Ratner went to work in his father's jewellery business at seventeen as a shop salesman. In 1984, aged 35, he was appointed managing director. Fiercely acquisitive, Ratners now has a quarter of the British jewellery market, piling its products high and selling them cheaply. Ratners would like to achieve the same result in the United States.

My biggest mistake was withdrawing from the Gordons deal. Back in November 1988 we had made the Zales (UK) and Salisbury acquisitions, and because we issued shares to acquire them, we gave an undertaking to our shareholders not to do any more for the foreseeable future. So when Gordons came up we weren't in a position to issue paper to buy it.

Gordons was losing money, but it was the second biggest jeweller in America, with 600 shops, many freehold or on cheap rents, and it had no debt. We'd already bought Sterling in the United States and two other chains, so we already had about 350 shops. At $500,000 (£300,000) a store, Gordons was unbelievably cheap.

Gordons announced publicly it was for sale and immediately our shares dropped 10p. But we looked at buying it with preference shares and cash. We were going to raise $300m, or £200m sterling. We calculated conservatively that we could make £60m out of Gordons in the first year, with £20m to pay in interest, so that would equal an earnings enhancement for the group of about £40m – quite unbelievable. I flew over to America and told the Gordon family we'd pay $39 a share. (They'd told me there was another party prepared to pay $38; I thought it was Kays, another big US jeweller.) I flew back to London and our shares had gone even lower, and I had messages to phone various people in the City. They said, Gerald, we strongly advise you to forget it, you will be treated like a leper.

I was shaken. Also, I had made the mistake of not consulting with all of my board at the time – not very tactful. So we had a board meeting and I informed the board that I'd been advised that our shares would go down quite dramatically. But, I said, we're only in the jewellery business, and we can't expand any more in the UK. If we're going to achieve domination in the US market, we've got to do it.

But some of the staff had share options, and the thing that frightened them was purely that they would lose money. Some of the board were against it and there was also a feeling that Gordons would be around next year. Kays and Zales Corp, our US competitors, both had huge debt, so we didn't think they'd buy it. So we called the whole thing off.

I could have argued it if I hadn't been shaken a bit. But I was influenced by everybody for the first time.

That evening our American president and finance director arrived because we were going to announce the deal the next morning. I had to meet them at the airport and tell them it was off, to their total disbelief. But two days later we changed our minds again and decided to go ahead with it. I rang Gordons and they said, What are you playing at? The next morning I got a phone call to say that Zales Corp, our biggest competitor, had purchased Gordons for $36.75. Gordons had thought we were going to drop out again.

We had just replaced Zales as the top jeweller in the US, but this saved them totally. Not only did we lose the deal, but that deal transformed our biggest competitor.

I've learnt not to listen to other people, who are generally nervous. If you feel that something is the right decision, you should really go ahead with it.

Obviously you listen, but if you're the managing director of a company, you have got to make the decision yourself.

It's no good complaining that the City doesn't want you to do something – it's the same thing as complaining that a customer won't buy your product. It's your job to make that product so irresistible that they'll buy it. I didn't do that.

4 February 1990

Richard Branson

At 39, Richard Branson is one of Britain's best-known, least conventional businessmen. He started as a schoolboy publisher before moving into selling cut-price records by mail order. The Virgin empire now includes Britain's second largest long-haul airline, Virgin Atlantic, and Virgin Records, one of the world's largest record companies.

My biggest mistake was being too awe-struck by my bank and staying with it after Virgin had grown too big. It led to a nightmare which nearly put us out of business and reveals a great deal about how short-sighted some British bankers are.

It happened in 1984, the year we launched Virgin Atlantic. Coutts & Co, whom I had been with since I was fifteen, were our bankers. Virgin was now their second biggest client after the Queen. In the very early days back in the 1960s Virgin staff used to walk in barefoot to put money into the bank, and although by this time the company had a turnover of £110m and was making £11m profit, Coutts never realized we had grown up and were now among the ten top private companies in the country. Neither had I realized it was time for us to move on.

Our overdraft at Coutts was £3m, and when we launched the airline we asked for an increase to £4m. We had limited the risk through a deal with Boeing which allowed us to return the first 747 at the end of the year if it did not work. But Coutts completely panicked and refused to raise the limit.

It wouldn't have mattered except that the day before our inaugural flight to the US, disaster struck. On the final check flight to get our airworthiness certificate from the Civil Aviation Authority, a bird flew into one of the engines. I remember it because I was sitting next to the CAA inspector as the plane took off when there was a tremendous bang and flash of flames from one of the engines. The CAA was very sympathetic but our engine insurance did not take effect until we had our certificate and there was £600,000 of damage. We did the inaugural flight on a spare engine but the expense meant we were likely to go £200,000 over our overdraft.

When I arrived home from the US exhausted after a successful first flight, I found my bank manager on my doorstep. I will remember that day for the rest of my life. He said he came with instructions that if we went 1p over our overdraft they would bounce our cheques. I took him to the door and told him he was not welcome in my house.

That weekend we rang up our foreign companies to try to get cash in. Coutts would not offset money we had overseas against our overdraft. We even had $6m due in from MGM for a film deal which would have wiped out the overdraft. But they were still threatening to put 2,500 Virgin staff on the streets. They did in fact bounce a couple of cheques. But by Tuesday we had enough money in from abroad.

After that, I finally plucked up courage to visit some other banks. We soon found three prepared to lend us £30m and then raised £35m in redeemable preference shares from the City. (Later that same year the CBI, *Sunday Telegraph*, Lloyds Bank and Barclays chose us as Company of the Year.) Within two years we went public, with a value placed on the company of £240m.

Five years later the group has a turnover of more than £1bn, employs over 5,000 people in 30 countries, has fifteen banks of different nationalities and a £300m overdraft limit.

It turned out all right for us. But there are a lot of companies with good ideas that are closed down because banks don't understand the business. Most banking nightmare stories are never told, because people cannot afford to risk offending their banks.

The problem with the British banking system is that clearing banks train people to be conservative and unadventurous, whereas in countries like West Germany, banks take stakes in business. I think British banks have more to worry about from the single European market than perhaps any other industry.

28 January 1990

Sir Roy Strong

Sir Roy Strong became director of the Victoria and Albert in 1974, at 38. He remained there until 1987. He is known for his trenchant views and does nothing to avoid controversy. His period at the V & A was marked by several stormy episodes reflecting his battles with government and unions over staffing and finance for the arts. Since leaving the museum, Sir Roy has continued his career as a historian and art critic, as well as being a prolific writer and broadcaster. He is an expert on gardens and has published several books on the subject.

Cutting the regional service of the Victoria and Albert Museum was one of the most painful episodes I have lived through, and I hope I never have to face anything like it again.

It all started in May 1976. I had been head of the museum for two years, the youngest director ever to have been appointed. I had been brought in, among other things, to modernize the regional exhibition service, which supplies material and expertise to local museums and colleges. I had also been told that I would have more or less unlimited resources to do so.

It was therefore a shock when I and the head of the Science Museum – Margaret Weston – were called into the Department of Education and Science and told to carry out an exercise on the effect of cutting our staffs by 10, 15 and 20 per cent. As parts of the DES, we were having to shoulder the department's staff reductions. And we were told to say nothing. I felt utterly betrayed.

I have always believed that what you do, you do well. I could have cut a bit of every department of the V & A , and this is actually what the unions wanted when they finally heard about the plans. But instead I decided to announce the cutting of one whole department – the V & A's regional exhibition service.

It was a deliberate gamble. The service was world renowned, there was nothing to equal it, and it had been running for more than 100 years. It was the model for similar services all around the world. I believed a Labour government would never allow it to be closed down if only because popular outrage would prevent it.

In November that year I gathered the entire V & A staff – more than 700 people all told – into the museum's Raphael Cartoon Court and had to tell them about the cut. Then ensued the most fantastic row. The regions, the staff and the unions were all up in arms about it. The metropolitan authorities kicked up a fuss, there was confrontation with the unions, and fury from the public. It was, after all, the height of union power at this time and the bargaining sessions I had with their representatives were bitter.

The issue was never out of the papers over the next few months. I was alone and, as a civil servant, unable to express any opinion. It was a desperately unhappy time; my hair turned white.

Shirley Williams, who was Secretary of State for Education at the time, took no interest in any of this until she suddenly realized that it was becoming an issue in the House. The unions appealed to her over my head.

Yet in the end I turned out to be wrong: I had mistakenly thought the Government would never let the regional department go, but they did. And what made it all the worse was that at the cost of losing this priceless service, the DES only saved about £250,000.

Good always comes out of bad, however, and the trauma helped me to push the rest of the antiquated V & A into the modern world.

Moreover, it turned out that I had been right in choosing to preserve the heart of the museum. A few years later the Tories ordered further cuts at the V & A which would have been even more damaging if I had already weakened the museum in 1976. Nevertheless, the strife caused by all this took up five years of my directorship. It demoralized the place and led to further problems with the unions. But no one at the DES cared a damn.

25 March 1990

Part Two

Personnel Mistakes

One of the biggest stumbling blocks for British executives continues to be the management of people.

By comparison, strategic and financial issues can be fairly straightforward – partly because they can be seen in the abstract. The problem with employees is that they are real and are not always predictable.

The cynical might say that this is behind the trend to talk about human resources rather than personnel – as if the difficulty could be dealt with by pretending that it isn't there. But treating people as if they are just another resource, like fuel or raw materials, is to miss the point.

People are a resource. But, with the decline of traditional industries, such as manufacturing, and the rise of the service company, they are more important than just about every other component of the organization. And at a time when many operations are undergoing massive changes in the effort to compete on a global scale understanding staff motivations, concerns and needs is more important than ever.

A few of the contributors collected in this section confess to problems in conveying the idea of change. For example, Paul Layzell, who ran BMW's British import subsidiary at the height of its success in the late 1980s, admitted that he should have realized sooner the need for change, 'so that our people lower down the organization could contribute more'.

On the other hand, British Steel chairman Sir Robert Scholey says his biggest mistake was to believe that you can get people to understand – and agree to – massive changes. 'If a company is enjoying a profitable niche in a healthy market you can afford to have consensus management. But if the ship's taking in water you just can't have a meeting on the poop deck to discuss whether to man the pumps,' he says, suggesting that the management has to take a lead or have change forced on it.

This experience was born of a national steel strike in 1980. And personnel matters have certainly historically been tied up with industrial relations. Strikes and the like are now few and far between, but it was not always that way, particularly in the car industry, as two contributors from different sides of the fence recall.

Geoff Whalen, who went on to become managing director of rival car maker Peugeot Talbot, says his mistake was in believing that what he calls institutionalized industrial democracy could work at the then British Leyland. The problem was that in 1975 relations between the management and the workers were in such a bad way that, although industrial democracy was demanded by the company's new owner (the State), it stood little chance of success.

Matters at the company had not apparently improved too much a couple of years later, when union leader Bill Jordan says he made his biggest mistake. Derek (Red Robbo) Robinson was dismissed after choosing to fight proposals involving widespread redundancies and radical changes to working practices that the workforce had reluctantly accepted. Mr Jordan's error was to misunderstand the mood of his members and to realize too late that they would not accept his call for Mr Robinson's reinstatement because they knew that the way things were done had to change.

But personnel-related mistakes need not be so momentous. They can apply to a particular individual. And several of the contributors have admitted to such personal failings as arrogance, not being prepared to delegate, inattention to detail, even name-dropping.

This being the time when total quality is a concept on everybody's lips if not yet in their minds, it is perhaps not surprising that customer satisfaction and client care rear their heads.

Dennis Kennedy of control systems makers Honeywell says that he was like many other managers in thinking that customer satisfaction was 'the sole preserve of the sales and marketing department'. Now, of course, he realizes it applies to the whole company.

Likewise, advertising agency chief executive Andrew Robertson confesses his mistake was to underestimate the amount of intensive care that a major client needed. 'When the relationship with a client isn't strong it is essential to check and double-check that they are happy with the progress that is being made,' he says. Incidentally, the current management teaching insists that this should be done even where the relationship is felt to be strong.

So is all this side of things just a collection of faddish concepts that cannot really be taught? In other words, are managers not just born with 'people skills' rather than trained in them?

Brewer Anthony Fuller's experience suggests otherwise. His big regret in his time at the family firm is that he has received no real training. 'Throughout the 27 years that I have been here I have flown by the seat of my pants,' he says. 'In business you are doing that with a lot of things, but to run a company that way is wrong,'

But there are some things that no amount of training can prepare you for. For instance, it cannot have been lack of attention to courses that led to accountant Chris Swinson turning up a day early to temporarily replace a financial management team that had not yet been removed. It was a simple human error – trusting in relayed messages. He says he has learned his lesson and now double-checks everything. But he must have gained an insight into how those managers felt when, earlier this year, he was ousted from his position as national managing partner of BDO Binder Hamlyn.

And prominent trade unionist Clive Jenkins sounds as if he is daily haunted by what he claims is his biggest mistake. Asked by a radio producer to suggest somebody to provide a point of view different from his own, he came up with the name of Norman Tebbitt, now Lord Tebbitt, but then a newly elected MP. Rather like Frankenstein and his monster, he says his error was in not knowing what he was going to turn into.

Anthony Cleaver

As chairman and CEO of IBM United Kingdom Holdings, Tony Cleaver presides over a company with a current turnover of £4.5bn, employing 18,500. Born in 1938, he joined the company as a trainee instructor, after graduation from Trinity College, Oxford. His career took him to the US and Paris before he became CEO in 1986, achieving the chairmanship this year. He is a non-executive director of General Accident, and other strings to his bow include membership of the CBI President's Committee and the British Overseas Trade Board. He is on the board of the English National Opera. He is married with one son.

My biggest mistake was in failing to appreciate the external value of the skills that our people possess. Let me explain. In 1986 I took over as chief executive officer of IBM (UK). In common with the rest of the industry, we had enjoyed a period of outstanding growth in the first half of the 1980s. This had been fuelled by a number of developments, of which the most dramatic had been the emergence of the personal computer. However, by the end of 1985 it was clear this growth was slowing and our customers were beginning to look for more than simply higher-performance hardware and software.

In the next two years, we analysed our organization and came to the conclusion that one of our major problems was that we had become top-heavy and that too few of our people were really close to our customers in understanding and responding to their requirements.

As a result, we transferred about 750 people from head office and support departments into field marketing branches. This transition proved very successful, with almost all of those transferred making a positive contribution and being welcomed by the customers and their marketing colleagues alike.

It was at this point that I began to realize just how foolish we had been in under-estimating the skills these people possess. In the internal departments where they had worked, they had been trained in the use of our systems and techonology as applied to their particular functions, be it accounting, administration, property management or whatever. And it was this combination of functional expertise and understanding how to apply technology to it that was so valuable.

Today, while we continue the process of transferring people, we have moved on to a second stage, where a large number of our employees remain in their support departments but spend a significant amount of time working directly with our customers, thus bringing our latest experience directly into our customers' offices. Obviously, the starting point was our own information systems organization, and today we provide consultancy and implementation assistance on all areas, from application justification to machine-room operations.

The process has also spread much wider. As our customers increasingly look for total solutions, we have gone as far for one retail company client as locating, designing, building and equipping complete computer suites, using the skills of our property department.

The latest development has been to apply this approach to a number of our people who have chosen to take early retirement but whose skills are still valuable to us and to our customers. We have helped to found a new company which those retiring early can join, with a guarantee of a number of days' work paid for by us over the first two years. This enables them to make the transition from full-time employment more easily, and means we retain access to their experience.

Looking back, it is perhaps ironic that having been brought up in a company which has set such store by the value of its people, I was not quicker to realize that in the transition from a hardware-dominated business these people would provide the key to our future success. We could have started much faster, simply by providing better access to our internal skills even before redeployment. Had we had the confidence in the skills of our people that we should have had we would have progressed much faster towards becoming the solutions company we are seeking to be.

22 July 1990

Sir Robert Scholey

Sir Robert Scholey, 68, grew up and was educated in Sheffield, where he started in the engineering profession. He has spent his whole working life in the steel industry, and has won international plaudits for his management of British Steel through the bad days of nationalization, recession and strikes to reprivatization and its current high profitability. Currently chairman of the company, he is also a director of the Eurotunnel board, a non-executive director of the National Health Service Policy Board and chairman of the Ironbridge Gorge Museum Development Trust.

My biggest mistake was to believe that you can get people to understand when you need to make massive changes and agree to them. That belief was gained in part from my early days at the United Steel Companies in the 1960s, where we were able to manage change by getting a reasonable degree of understanding from the workforce.

Then we were nationalized by the Wilson government in 1967. A whole group of different companies and cultures was amalgamated into the British Steel Corporation, just as the boom in steel demand faded.

Questioning the future shape of the corporation, we concluded that its objective should be to make itself a modern, competitive force in the world of steel. There was political support for investment, but there were social difficulties in closing old plants. But it was quite clear, if one looked at our competitors – especially Japan – we had to change.

This was during the mid-1970s, when I was chief executive. Monty Finneston was chairman, and he took a tough line with the unions with respect to seeking change. Lots of old plants had to close and we had to do better with what we had. We had a manpower level of 250,000, and the losses were fairly enormous. Even the Wilson government which returned in 1974 found our losses too big a burden to be carried.

I felt it was possible to change people's views if they saw what we were up against. Sir Charles Villiers, who became chairman in 1976 was of the same view. I had already taken the trade union leaders to Japan to see what the competition was like. As was the practice at the time, we took them through the same papers that went before the board, too, so they had all the financial details before them. In private we could get them to acknowledge what it was about, but beyond that they refused to budge.

By this stage, the losses were intolerable. We were getting to the crunch point. By 1979 we were looking for a reduction of 50,000 of the workforce. But the uneconomic situation of the company became obfuscated by a row over a pay deal we were offering, which included a productivity element for the first time. On 2 January 1980 we plunged into a national steel strike lasting three months.

I had failed to persuade the unions of the need to change without industrial action. At the end of the strike, steel production was down by 100,000 tonnes a week and we lost a lot of business. Ultimately 100,000 workers had to leave the industry, and although today we are a highly profitable company, our market share has never been fully retrieved. Our position as a major player in Europe was reduced significantly and we've not been able to remedy that.

It's still tempting to think that if everybody had been rational in outlook and managed their affairs properly, we could have made those changes without all the pain and loss. But now I don't believe it can be done like that. If a company is enjoying a profitable niche in a healthy market you can afford to have consensus management. But if the ship's taking in water you just can't have a meeting on the poop deck to discuss whether to man the pumps. The lesson I learned is one that applies to this country and its industry just as much as it did to British Steel. It's a big mistake to think you're ever going to explain and get everyone to agree changes necessary to deliver the economic growth the country needs. If the situation isn't to get worse you have to go ahead and make the necessary changes. If you don't, then in the end change is forced on you anyway and it's usually worse.

29 July 1990

Dennis Kennedy

> Dennis Kennedy, 55, was born and educated in Scotland, where he trained as an engineer. He began his industrial career with Honeywell, the controls systems manufacturer, in 1960. He moved to GEC and then on to ITT for thirteen years, working in the US, UK and Europe. In 1982 he ran Veeder Root and then moved to Qume Corporation, both in America. Finally he returned in 1989 to Britain and Honeywell. In January 1990 he took over as chairman and managing director, and is a vice-president of Honeywell, Europe.

My biggest mistake was believing that customer satisfaction was the sole preserve of the sales and marketing department. Like many managers, I had partitioned in my mind the various functions in the business, such as manufacturing, finance, distribution and, of course, sales and marketing. Customers always talked first to the sales and marketing staff, who were expected to handle complaints. Inside the company there was a tendency to focus on product quality, because we believed, mistakenly as it turned out, that faulty products were the biggest source of those complaints.

In 1982, I became president of an old-established American company which produced controls, instruments and counters and sold them internationally. At the time, our cost of quality was becoming an increasingly large proportion of the cost of selling products to customers. We were dealing with problems that arose after making the sale, rather than trying to prevent them from happening. We started with a cost control exercise, but we soon realized that the problem was much more significant in terms of overall customer service. We found that 87 per cent of customer complaints were to do with items other than product quality or delivery: for example, documentation, instruction manuals, faulty invoicing, and so on.

Between 1982 and 1986, we changed the system completely, so that everyone in the company realized that we were all responsible for satisfying our customers. The internal cost of quality was ultimately reduced by 50 per cent and the total number of complaints was cut by 80 per cent. When I came to Honeywell in 1989, I found the company in the midst of a similar process. Again it needed to be emphasized that customer satisfaction did not come from one department – sales and marketing – but from the whole company.

For example, we have a division which supplies control systems to companies engaged in the manufacture of gas boilers for residential heating systems. The sales responsibility in the UK is separate from the engineering and manufacturing operation and the distribution centre, which are all in the Netherlands. Yet customers only had access to the company through sales, so their enquiries followed a tortuous route around the company.

I know from my personal experience as a customer how frustrating it is when you purchase something and there's a problem – as when you take a half-day off work to take delivery of your purchase and the delivery men don't turn up. Or you ring the supplier to find out when your purchase will be ready, and you get pushed around on the telephone and fobbed off. I realized that it was just the same for our customers.

Now we've changed the process in that Honeywell division, so that customers can go directly to the relevant function and talk about their needs. We're doing much better already, although we've still got a long way to go – but then it's a never-ending process.

So I learned from my mistake. Today I know about our customers' complaints and I read those that are addressed to my desk. I make sure they are followed up, we have a system in place that ensures that they are dealt with properly, and, where appropriate, I call the customer afterwards. All my directors and senior managers deal with customers on that personal basis. Now everyone in the organization understands that we are all responsible for keeping our customers satisfied.

5 August 1990

Sir David Plastow

Sir David Plastow, 58, was born in Grimsby, Lincolnshire, and educated at Culford School in Suffolk. At eighteen he joined Vauxhall Motors as an apprentice, moving to Rolls-Royce in 1958. He became managing director in 1972. In 1975, he became non-executive director of Vickers and was named the *Guardian* Young Businessman of the Year. In 1980, he became chief executive of the merged Vickers and Rolls-Royce Motors, adding the role of chairman seven years later. Sir David is a patron of the Samaritans and Fellow of the Royal Society of Arts.

My biggest mistake was keeping a particular board structure beyond its useful life, instead of changing it promptly. The board structure was born of the marriage between Vickers and Rolls-Royce Motors in 1980. I had been managing director of Rolls-Royce and a non-executive director of Vickers, so I knew something of the Vickers culture.

Clearly, after the merger, we had an enormous task to get this new company into shape, particularly as it had to be able to cope with the emerging economic threats of the time.

After a thorough review of our strategy we decided that unless we had manufacturing businesses that were truly capable of competing on international terms we would have to get rid of them.

Certain things had to be put into place, such as faster financial reporting, and cultural changes had to be made to improve internal communications and break down unnecessary status barriers.

We also decided to have large chunks of the business represented at board level by 'barons', in other words, by managers of the operating divisions. Assets would be represented proportionally on the board, some two-thirds from Vickers, one-third from Rolls-Royce.

But I began to realize that the effectiveness of the barons suffered from the dichotomy of the role. They were always fighting their own corners. Their first preoccupation was their own particular empire so it was very difficult for them to think corporately.

Yet at board level the responsibility must be to take care of the corporate business as a whole and maintain earnings per share growth as a whole. There may be people who can do both simultaneously but they are thin on the ground. By 1984, it was evident that we needed to strip the board of people who were committed to their empires.

But I delayed making the change. It was partly because of a sense of commitment to undertakings made at the time of the merger. But I suppose it was also a lack of courage on my part. It is very hard to look a man in the eye and tell him something like that. The most painful process in business life at any level is to be party to cutting staff . . . and requires the deepest thought and responsibility. You get no praise for it and it is certainly not a macho thing to be bragged about. Yes, we lost some good people, and we don't talk about it in the company now, some things are best left unsaid.

I felt at the time that I needed to establish the rationale in everyone's mind before making this major change. I made the change eventually but I should have done it quickly, in the first two years.

Since 1984 we have had an executive board which consists of the managing director, myself as chief executive and nowadays chairman, together with the finance director and the commercial director. We have sold 35 different operations, bought several companies, and reduced gearing from 55 per cent in the early 1980s to zero.

Ultimately the barons had acted as buffers between us and the business. Now, if one of our senior managers wants to make an acquisition, or some other significant move, we have his team's prospectus by Friday and he is in my office on Monday, putting the case directly to the board.

We can come to a conclusion very quickly and make a decision because there is just one body for companies to approach, not layers of committees. It is a structure that serves Vickers well.

23 September 1990

George Bain

Professor George Bain, 51, is principal of the London Business School. A Canadian, he attended the University of Manitoba before taking a D.Phil. in industrial relations at Oxford University. A long association with the University of Warwick culminated in his term as chairman of the School of Industrial and Business Studies from 1983 to 1989. His many books and papers on industrial relations have given him an international reputation and he has mediated in numerous disputes.

I made my biggest mistake when I was at the University of Warwick. I may have made worse mistakes than this one, but as they chiefly concerned people – hiring decisions and the like – they are probably best left alone. I took over as chairman of the School of Industrial and Business Studies in 1983, and the place began to expand quite rapidly. Perhaps belonging to the art-as-wallpaper school, I decided to get some art to cover the blank walls. Being a believer in participative management, I brought up for discussion at the executive committee of the business school the idea that we should use some of our surplus funds to purchase works of art. Well, this opened up the biggest can of worms imaginable. There was a long-running debate and considerable conflict.

People fell into three camps. First, there were those who represented the art-as-an-investment school. They argued for buying Japanese prints because they would appreciate in value. Second, there were the supporters of local artists. Coventry College of Further Education had an art school and these people felt that we should be supporting young local artists. (My secretary actually paid about £90 for some things from the art school to show that the idea had had some consideration.) Third, there was the art-as-reality school. This held that reality could only truly be captured by photographs. As a result, supporters of this idea felt that we should buy photographs.

What I thought was going to be an isssue that would go through on the nod ran and ran. It went on for eighteen months to two years and was using up considerable managerial time. Consequently, I decided to drop the whole issue. I waited for the dust to settle and then my secretary borrowed some fine art catalogues from a local gallery and went out and bought a number of pictures for the board room. And the whole thing quietly went away. One thing it demonstrated is that the less important the topic is the greater will be the discussion.

My mistake was in the way that I handled it. In taking up an issue of that kind – in which there is no obvious objective criterion – for discussion, any hope that you are going to get agreement on it is forlorn. I should have known that on something like this, with academics involved, I was asking for trouble. I was a victim of my enthusiasm for participation.

My field is industrial relations – I have spent my whole life examining trade unions and industrial conflict. With something like a wage dispute, there is room for compromise. The two sides start with conflicting offers and can usually work towards agreement.

Where I went wrong was in trying to transfer what works in one situation to another without realizing that it doesn't necessarily work for that situation. Taste is like a dictatorship and discussion is not a mechanism for bridging a conflict of this kind.

However, I have learned my lesson. I became principal of the London Business School last summer and we have been having a discussion about our address. At the moment, the address is the London Business School, Sussex Place, Regents Park, London NW1, and there has been a suggestion that we should drop the Sussex Place and just have our address as the London Business School, Regents Park, London NW1. When the subject came up for discussion, we talked about it for half an hour and I then accepted a motion to guillotine it.

2 December 1990

Anthony Fuller

Anthony Fuller, 50, is chairman and managing director of Fuller Smith & Turner, the family controlled brewers based in Chiswick, west London. His family has been involved in running the business for six generations. He was awarded the CBE for his work as chairman of the Brewers' Society – a post he held from 1986 to 1989, two years longer than the normal term because of the Monopolies and Mergers Commission's review of the industry. His hobbies are shooting and deer stalking in Scotland.

My biggest mistake was basically having no real training. I had been at school, taken a short-service commission in the army and wandered around the world – and then I came here.

I was given what was considered to be the traditional family training, which was eighteen months going round various departments. Then I was put on to the property side as a sort of semi-surveyor dealing with the decorations and alterations to our pubs.

When I inquired of the people who were then in charge of the company, 'wouldn't it make sense to go to other companies and find out how other people did things', I was told that there was no need to do that. Fullers knew how to run its business and this was the way it had always been done. I regret not putting my foot down and saying that I should have done some proper training.

Throughout the 27 years that I have been here I have flown by the seat of my pants. In business you are doing that with a lot of things, but to run a company that way is wrong. The same thing happened when I went over to the wine side of the business. I was told to get on and run it.

Other than drinking a lot of wine, I did not know anything about it. The attitude was very inward-looking. It was: 'We know what we're doing.' All this has totally changed. The younger generation wants to go on courses. And if they don't, they get a shove from me. That's because of my experience. The approach is the same throughout the company. Fullers is still a family-controlled business. Although it is a public company on the Unlisted Securities Market, the three families – the Fullers, Smiths and Turners – control more than 70 per cent of it. The Smiths are dying out, but most of the directors are Fullers or Turners. Of the Turners, one came in as a solicitor and looks after the company's legal affairs. Another is a qualified accountant. He took over the wine side of the business and had to go on courses to learn about retailing. Now he has moved on to the marketing side and has had to learn about that. It is not so much going back to school as going on day courses.

The younger Fuller in the business is about 30 and was sent away to various other breweries to learn about how they do things, such as the managed house side and marketing, for several months before coming back here. My 22-year-old son is a stockbroker and says he wants to make his career in the City. I would like him to come into the business, but at the same time I am happy for him to gain experience outside.

In the meantime, we are doing quite well. We have acquired a good image for our beers, such as ESB and London Pride, and what we call the post-MMC era is proving to be very good for us. The fact that the big brewers have had to sell off pubs has enabled us to expand while our sales have been increasing very fast through the requirement that the big brewers have to sell guest beers in their pubs.

10 February 1991

Bill Jordan

> Bill Jordan, 54, is leader of the AEU, Britain's largest manufacturing trade union. He was born in Birmingham and at fifteen trained as a machine tool fitter. He first became active in unions at Guest Keen & Nettleford as a shop steward. By 1977, he was full-time West Midlands divisional organizer of the AEU (then AUEW). In 1986, he was elected president of the AEU. He has played an influential role in shaping modern unionism and is a governor of the BBC, Manchester Business School and LSE.

I made my mistake during the Derek (Red Robbo) Robinson dismissal saga at British Leyland's Longbridge plant.

Michael Edwardes had been put in to British Leyland in 1977 to try to save it from collapse. With the election of a Conservative Government in 1979 it was generally believed he was empowered to reform BL or close it. The Draconian plans he drew up for the company meant wholesale redundancies and radical changes in working practices.

These were reluctantly accepted by the workforce in a ballot vote. But a group led by Derek Robinson, the Longbridge plant convener and senior AEU shop steward, chose to fight the proposals and the company decided to sack him.

The workforce's reaction to the dismissal gave the first indication that the old order was beginning to break down. While many departments had walked out, others stayed in – and ominously one shop steward said his department 'was still cheering the news'.

The AEU's executive council ordered a return to work while an investigation into Derek's dismissal took place. This showed conclusively that he had been unfairly dismissed.

I, as senior AEU official for the West Midlands, was given the job, along with Derek and the other union leaders involved, of taking the argument for the defence of his job to a mass meeting of the 15,000 workforce. This was my greatest responsibility to date, since the outcome of this meeting would certainly influence the climate of British industrial relations for some time to come. So I worked painstakingly on a detailed case for Derek's reinstatement.

I travelled to that meeting on Wednesday, 20 February 1980, confident that my catalogue of facts and figures would convince even the most cynical doubter of the need to defend Derek. But as I mounted the speakers' platform and stared across an endless sea of faces, I realized my mistake. I was trying to use a detailed argument to overturn a simple truth that those listening already knew.

I started to speak from my notes, through an ill-sounding tannoy system, my attention distracted by a chanting group holding a model gallows from which Derek's effigy was unmistakably hanging. I began to feel despair that I had not only misjudged the nature of the speech, but I had no plan B to fall back on. I kept on reading, but as I turned to page four of my notes it fluttered to the ground, and I wished I could have followed.

At the end of the meeting the workforce rejected us. They were not just voting to see Derek Robinson dismissed, they were signalling to the world that they knew the way things were done in their plant had to change. The AEU's president at the time, Terry Duffy, was wise enough to know that this was really about whether BL was to have a future or close, and he had given the final say to the only people who mattered – the workforce. My mistake, calamitous as it seemed to me at the time, taught me the need on momentous occasions to stick to simple truths.

17 February 1991

Joe Mcnally

Joe McNally, the 47-year-old head of Compaq Computer, made a bad error of judgement during his brief spell in the meat industry. Brought up and educated in Tyne and Wear, he went into the family business only to be fired by his father. He then worked for fifteen years with ICL and Honeywell, before moving to FMC-Harris, the meat business, for four years. Returning to the computer industry, he founded Compaq's UK subsidiary in 1984. It announced sales of over $1bn (£523m) for 1990.

My worst mistake in business happened to when I was running the Southern operations of FMC-Harris, the meat slaughtering, butchering and bacon business.

I had spent fifteen years in the computer industry where promotion to the senior jobs tended to come via sales and marketing and I wanted to gain more general management experience. So I took a job as managing director of a computer subsidiary at FMC-Harris.

Eventually I was appointed as one of the three operational chief executives in the main group, running the £130m southern division with some 20 plants.

The problem with the fresh meat business is that it doesn't profitably add value. The margins get squeezed between the farmers and the supermarkets and in any case there is overcapacity in the sector.

Although we were the largest in our sector our margins were deplorable – less than 10 per cent before expenses. The plant overheads were very high and large parts of the business were running at a loss.

I knew that the only way to make money was to run a very lean operation with tight cost controls. A high proportion of our costs was labour, which was heavily unionized. Over the years the rates for things such as overtime, shiftwork and dirty work, such as slaughtering, were absolutely astronomic. I knew we had to cut them.

But I wasn't a meat man and the market had generally been run by traditional commodity traders just as it had been for 30 years. Even though we were in so much trouble, the advice given by these experienced managers was that I couldn't do it.

I was persuaded, much against my better judgement, that if I cut the rates the union would call a strike and walk out. If that happened the factories had such huge overheads that we would have been forced to shut them and that would have led to closing down half the business.

In the short term interest of keeping the business going, I followed this advice. Maybe what I should have done was follow Mrs Thatcher's line and say to hell with it because in the long term the damage was irreparable. We lost several millions and a year later, by which time I was identified as group chief executive designate, we were forced to sell the business to Hillsdown at a knockdown price. But it taught me a lesson I'll never forget.

Now I am very aware that in Compaq I have an extremely fast-growing, profitable business but that its growth must slow as the UK personal computer market reaches saturation. I can't afford to spend all my time worrying about the short term. I now spend most of my time thinking about the long term, and in particular, the medium term consolidation and creation of markets.

The problem with FMC-Harris was that someone had to renegotiate the rates with the unions at some point. Not doing so was one of the factors which damaged the business and led to its sale. What I try to do now is think about the problems before they happen, not tackle them when it is too late.

3 March 1991

Peter Gummer

Peter Gummer, 48, is chairman of Shandwick, now the world's largest public relations group, as well as a non-executive director of the London board of the Halifax Building Society, NHS and Arts Council. He regularly lectures on public relations around the world, but as his story relates, he hasn't always been such a good speaker. He was educated at Selwyn College, Cambridge, and after working on local newspapers held a number of PR posts before founding Shandwick in 1974. It now employs more than 2,000 people in 100 offices, earning fees in excess of £100m.

This is the sort of mistake that, even now, writing it down 25 or so years later, makes my hands sweat and my skin crawl, and the memory is such that I will never, ever let it happen again.

I was invited, in 1965, to make a speech in Brussels to a management conference. The speech was to be quite long – 90 minutes as I recall – to about 50 middle-to-top-ranking businessmen.

Secretly I thought: wasn't presentation the key skill in public relations? Couldn't I 'snow' my way through any minor difficulties, such as lack of knowledge?

I remember settling down in my hotel room the night before the talk and the conference organizer asking for my lecture notes. I mumbled something about 'participative conference techniques' and said I would send the notes to the delegates after synthesizing their views.

The memory of arriving and standing before those who had paid to listen to me has not been erased by the mists of time. It is etched in my mind as clearly as if it were yesterday.

In a blinding flash I realized that I was underprepared. The audience knew that, and that they knew more about my subject than I ever would. I was caught . . . red-handed.

The first fifteen minutes were long and terrible. I lost the audience mentally and even physically – several actually left the room. The balance of the lecture period stretched before me in an unfillable void. I remember thinking, if I can get through 45 minutes I will be very lucky. I only just made it. I tried everything to recoup the situation. I asked them to participate, to share their experiences, to ask questions – of me, of each other. Anything. Nothing worked. Halfway through the session I called it a day, went meekly back to my hotel and nursed my injured pride. Mistakes like that arise from personal failings – in my case, arrogance. I believed that I could, by force of personality and persuasion, bluff my way through a lack of knowledge. My audience saw straight through me and made me suffer for my sins.

Never, never again. Going back on the plane I decided to write down why I did that so badly and what I could do to prevent any recurrence. This is what I wrote:

First, I cared more about what I wanted to say than they wanted to hear. Ask yourself who the audience is and what they want from your session.

Second, I didn't have enough material. You must have at least three times as much material as you will need, because something will go wrong and you will always have to dig into that reserve pot.

Third, I didn't prepare enough. As a rule of thumb, for every five minutes on your feet it will take 60 minutes of concentrated preparation and three full rehearsals.

Fourth, I wasn't flexible. I had no confidence in what I had to say, and so I couldn't adapt as the mood of the meeting changed.

Fifth, there is a dynamic to a live audience which you must learn to read.

Only experience, as I have since learnt, brings that.

That mistake changed my whole approach to speech-making – and indeed, presentations. I never do them casually, but work very hard at them and make sure no corners have been cut.

Once or twice, in recent years, family or colleagues have said how fortunate I am to be able to deliver speeches with such apparent ease. The reason is simple, and my palms are now sweating again as I think of it.

7 April 1991

Andrew Robertson

Andrew Robertson is chief executive of WCRS, the advertising agency. He grew up in Zimbabwe and South Africa and arrived in England aged eighteen intending to study civil engineering. But a temporary job on a cold, muddy building site in Windsor changed his mind and instead he read economics at City of London Polytechnic. His first job in advertising was as trainee media planner with Ogilvy & Mather. By 26 he had made it to the board as new business director. He moved to J Walter Thompson in 1989 as a group director and in November 1990, aged 30, was appointed chief executive of WCRS.

Oscar Wilde once said that experience is the name that people give to their mistakes, and on that basis I've had more experience than most in my nine years in the advertising business. But my worst professional mistake was underestimating the intensive care a major client needed.

It happened two years ago when I was 28 and moving to J Walter Thompson as one of the five group directors. Bacardi, which was a key UK account billing £5m per annum, had fired JWT that morning. JWT had managed to persuade them to stay the execution for four weeks, giving it a chance to put together new creative recommendations. The agency wanted me to lead the team doing the pitch, not least because I would be the only group director with no previous contact with the client.

I said yes, obviously, and we went and spent a considerable sum of agency money shooting some new pictures, and then made a big presentation to them on a Thursday. They told us at the start that they were not going to give us an answer there and then, but wanted to go away and discuss our proposals. They didn't ring until Friday at 4pm to tell us that we had kept the business. As you might imagine we had a very jolly Friday night. So we carried on much as usual. I started working with them properly on the 'Nothing feels like Bacardi' campaign. We had done some very stylish shots for their poster and press ads and spent five months developing a cinema campaign.

Then one day I got back to find a note on my desk from Miles Colebrook, chief executive of JWT Europe. I went to see him, only to hear that Bacardi had fired us. They had stipulated that there was nothing we could do and that they had already appointed Grey Advertising to the account. I couldn't believe it at first, but a minute after Miles said it I knew exactly why this had happened. Everybody involved tried to reason it out. In fact, it wasn't any particular thing, just that although we had persuaded them not to go, in six months we hadn't done enough to persuade them to stay.

It was as if somebody had climbed out on to a window ledge and threatened to jump. We had done a lot of talking and all they'd done was sit down. They hadn't jumped, but we hadn't managed to talk them inside; the problem was that we carried on working as if they were safely indoors.

When the relationship with a client isn't strong it is essential to check and double-check that they are happy with the progress that is being made. It is very hard for them to tell you that they're not. They've made a decision not to fire you and although they aren't really committed they feel they need to appear to be, so they bottle it all up and don't say anything. Meanwhile, you are going along happily believing you've salvaged it. From this I have learned never to heave a sigh of relief when we avoid something dreadful – all you've done then is get back to zero. You can only heave a sigh of relief when something's gone brilliantly.

It is a fundamental function of my job to make sure that my group directors, who are closest to the clients, are always stretching themselves and the agency on all pieces of business at all times. To do this I have to know what I'm talking about on each account. It's all about attention to detail. Our operating philosophy now is simple. We try to work on every account as if we were pitching for it every day.

26 May 1991

Sir Christopher Harding

Sir Christopher Harding, 51, is chairman of British Nuclear Fuels Ltd and vice-chairman of Hanson Transport Group. He graduated from Oxford with a degree in history before joining ICI in 1961, where he held various senior personnel management positions. In 1969 he joined Hanson plc. Initially he turned down the opportunity to become chairman of BNFL because he had never had a science lesson in his life and was terrified his lack of technical knowledge would be a problem. Six months later he was asked again, and this time he agreed.

There's no doubt I make mistakes every day of my life, but the one that left its biggest mark happened very early in my career and taught me the importance of paying attention to detail.

I had left university as an eager young graduate, keen to make a name for myself, and immediately joined ICI. I was the most junior person in the central staff department, and the senior manager was a perfectionist. He had a fearsome reputation for sorting out young graduates.

After about nine months, he called me into his office and said he was giving me a very responsible job to undertake.

The annual personnel directors conference was coming up. All the personnel directors and managers from every UK division of ICI were attending, and I was to handle the travel arrangements and administration.

It was in the days when the cold winds were blowing through ICI and all possible economies were being made.

The chauffeur-driven car fleet had been cut, so it was decided we should get everybody to assemble at headquarters and then transport them by coach to the company's staff college outside London.

I duly made the arrangements for two coaches to appear at 2.30pm in time for a prompt departure at 3pm. And on the day, there I was, surrounded by 60-odd people all waiting to board the coaches – which were nowhere in sight. At this point I was getting very nervous. I hadn't seen it as a particularly demanding assignment, but I wanted to pursue a career in personnel and I was very conscious that I was handling some of the most senior people in the company. People who were going to have some say in my future. The seconds ticked by and still the coaches didn't come. By 2.55pm my boss was asking some very pointed questions, and I disappeared to ring the coach company only to find that they hadn't even set off.

I was shattered, because I had spoken to them that morning to double-check the arrangements. It turned out that the person I had spoken to had looked up the wrong booking for the wrong day.

My boss tore me to pieces, and I was extremely embarrassed because not only had I let him down, but all those other people who were milling around. There was no satisfactory explanation I could give. He made it absolutely clear that not only should I have checked, but in order to be certain I should have gone to the garage and been on the first coach to make sure it arrived on time.

As it was, we had to rustle up as many cars as we could and book taxis for everyone else, so the whole operation cost considerably more than it should have done.

It taught me a lot about contingency plans. Not only should I have had a plan B, but to satisfy my boss I should certainly have had a plan C. He was kind enough to give me a second chance. But it left an indelible impression on me. It taught me that if something is important, you cannot rely on others to do exactly what you think you've agreed with them. You have to make quite sure they have the same understanding of what you think you have communicated.

Ever since, paying attention to detail has been extremely important to me. In fact this has led me to be something of a bore to my splendid secretaries who do not actually need me to triple-check all the arrangements they make on my behalf.

30 June 1991

Roy Watts

Roy Watts, 65, is chairman of Thames Water, Lowndes Lambert
Group and Frank Graham Group. Born in Doncaster, he served in the
Royal Tank Regiment from 1943 to 1947 and attended Edinburgh
University before entering local government as an accountant. After
five years he joined British European Airways in 1955. He held a
number of management posts with this company and its successor
British Airways, becoming chief executive in 1972 and combining
this role with that of chairman from 1974 until his departure for
Thames Water in 1983.

My mistakes have generally been about people – colleagues I should have
appointed, or fired or restrained. That restricts what I can say. I have no
complaints about career moves. I sometimes ask myself why I went into
local government after university and the army. I found it hard work,
though it proved good experience. It educated me in the control of
expenditure, which has stood me in good stead ever since. And it
provided – by chance – my opening in civil aviation, an industry that has
taken up the bulk of my working life – almost 30 years. So it must have
been a good move. I've always worked in big companies so I was not an
entrepreneur-gone-wrong. I have worked with people, through people,
for people, and in the process learned about people. As a consequence,
I'm suspicious of organizational change. Such change is often a substitute
for taking positive remedial decisions.

In the recession of 1980 I, like many in UK industry, should have begun
the retrenchment earlier. Whether I could have done so given the trade
union scene before Mrs Thatcher changed it, is open to question. There
would certainly have been a hell of a fight, even though I learned to
respect unions and ultimately found them sensible and co-operative if
issues were properly debated.

I learned that vertical integration is a luxury brought on by success, but
that in times of recession it becomes a millstone. I now prefer to have
competition among my suppliers.

As a young man I thought management was simply about carrots. I still
believe management is about leadership and example but I've come to
recognize the need for a stick also, and to realize that if you are

dissatisfied with a person's performance you act straightaway, and do not dither. What you learn, if nothing else, is that most decisions are about people, how they perform, how they react. Difficult decisions in business are about judgement. They will not be offered to you on a plate via a computer print-out.

The mistake that is perhaps my biggest falls into this area. It came in the 1970s, when I was working in aviation, for British Airways. I introduced club class in Europe and eliminated first class. The arguments were impeccable: a decline in first-class demand from 20 per cent of aircraft load to 2.5 per cent over 20 years. There was a growing impatience by business executives over conditions in the back of the aircraft. But we penny-pinched the change and annoyed a vociferous and influential minority. Today, there is no doubt about the success of club class, and nearly everybody in Europe has adopted it, but I should have listened more to the marketing people rather than to the planners at the start. I learned that change in business has to be led by customers' needs not the convenience of production. Fortunately, experience is the knowledge of precedent. That is why in Thames Water hose-pipe bans are seen to represent failure.

By contrast, the four domestic shuttles which I brought in from January 1975 were thoroughly researched, heavily resourced and progressively introduced. They turned aviation on its head.

The very idea of guaranteed unlimited seats and an airline standing by for its customers, rather than the other way round, sent a shiver through traditionalists from the board down. But it was right and it worked. It was about concept, not coffee.

7 July 1991

Lynne Franks

Lynne Franks, 43, is chairman of Lynne Franks PR, a consultancy she started in 1971. In those days she had just one client – fashion designer Katherine Hamnett. Today, the company has a staff of 60 and represents clients from a wide range of industries, including real estate, publishing, entertainment and design. In 1988, it was acquired by the Broad Street group. After restructuring, BDDP owns 75 per cent of the shares in the consultancy. Lynne Franks and husband Paul Howie hold the remaining 25 per cent. They received £6m from the deal.

It took me 20 years to realize that my biggest mistake was not trusting the people around me to do things they are perfectly capable of doing. When I first started the business, I worked on every single aspect of it – from bookkeeping to strategic planning and dealing with the press. Literally hours after the birth of my first child fifteen years ago, I was on the telephone to the office and talking to clients. It was the same two years later after the birth of my daughter.

Every time I went on holiday I spent at least two hours a day on the phone talking to the office, even if I was in Australia and it was the middle of the night.

Staying in touch made me feel that I was still in control.

The first turning point came a few years ago when I went away for Christmas. I arranged for the people in the office to cover the holiday period in case we had any queries and I rang in each day.

When we got back, my husband, who is the chief executive, asked if anyone had been ringing and the staff pointed out that the only person was me. It gradually occurred to me that I was completely ruining my holidays. I was not coming back relaxed and refreshed. Instead, I was getting tense over things I really could do nothing about. My health was suffering. I thought I was a machine that could just go on and on.

When you've built a company yourself, you're used to being involved in every little thing. I was at every new business meeting, every launch. And I'm a perfectionist, so it was terribly hard to learn to trust. But it is essential, because your business can't grow otherwise. It was my husband who pointed out that I could either run every aspect of a small business, or be chairman of a large, successful company employing excellent thinkers and operators in their own right.

When we first sold the business I was in major shock. I had always thought of it as mine and suddenly it wasn't. But I'm very happy about it now. Gradually, I have learnt that by surrounding myself with really capable people, I can let go.

It means that I can put my energies into the areas where I can be most effective because there are only so many hours in the day. It's terribly important that work is not all-consuming. It is a major part of my life, but so are my family and friends.

I've had to learn the difference between Lynne Franks, the person, and Lynne Franks PR, the company, because when you call a company by your own name, you can get very confused.

You have to get your ego into perspective.

The fact is, when people ring up and ask us to do their PR, they really are contacting the agency. Lynne Franks has come to mean so much more than me. It is about the energy and ideas of the 60 people who now work for the PR company.

Now I take time to go swimming or have a massage; or just find some time for myself. Not a lot, but enough. Because when I'm tired, I get negative; and then I get niggly.

In a company like Lynne Franks, the hours are long and stressful. But the staff have blossomed since I changed my attitude.

We've got four other directors, two of whom are only 27, and we have seven other senior managers.

It means that they are now working in a much more self-motivating atmosphere, and the business, as a result, has benefited.

11 August 1991

Paul Layzell

Paul Layzell, 50, ran BMW (GB), the most successful of the German car manufacturer's import subsidiaries, from 1984 to 1990. Under his leadership, BMW sales were doubled to nearly 50,000 a year in the UK, making it the largest European market for BMWs outside Germany itself. In his final year as managing director, profits rose by more than 400 per cent to £75m, on a turnover of £730m. He is now a director of Leadership Dynamics Europe, which specializes in assisting companies to effect and manage change in their corporate cultures.

My biggest mistake at BMW (GB) was in not realizing sooner the need for change so that our people lower down the organization could contribute more, for that's where the greatest untapped talent lay.

Although our sales and profitability at BMW (GB) had risen steadily throughout the 1980s, I decided in 1988 that the company culture required fundamental change. I had come to realize there was a huge gap between the organization we had and what it needed to be if our success was to continue. It meant challenging and perhaps changing the very things which had brought success in the past.

But because we were a top-performing company with spectacular growth in sales and profitability from marketing and distributing a prestigious product, I didn't question our management processes earlier. I should have. Our management structure was too hierarchical. There were too many layers of management, there was too much compartmentalization. Managers tended to be only interested in their own areas of responsibility. Teamwork was lacking. Too many of our headquarters staff were encouraged to pass decision-making upwards. Junior managers were often reluctant to make decisions for fear of making the wrong ones. Faced with a problem, they asked themselves: How would Paul Layzell tackle it?

Staff were confused as to their own role in the company. We were trapped in the day-to-day minutiae of measurement and control systems which reinforced the 'don't change' mentality.

It was clear that responsibility for making decisions needed to be devolved downwards. Too many people hung around waiting to be told what to do. Worse, they did no more than what they were told to do. I had been blind to one of the biggest obstacles – me. Our success had deceived me into thinking if I didn't do it myself, it wouldn't get done. I thought it was my job to create the agenda and then motivate 'them' to carry it out.

In the spring of 1989, during a visit to the US, I had a chance meeting with Ralph Stayer, who had made great strides in changing radically the culture of his own company, Johnsonville, a food manufacturer in Wisconsin. I learned from my discussions with Ralph that change cannot simply be ordered, without risking it being ignored by the very people who have to make it work.

On my return to the UK, we put together multidiscipline teams of people to identify what obstacles stood in the way of achieving 'customer delight' for BMW owners. We scrutinized all aspects of our business.

It emerged that our company priorities were not necessarily those held by our customers. So we started tracking the levels of customer satisfaction and awarded bonuses to those of our dealers who did best.

The whole process we went through at BMW (GB) taught me that change must be empowered and become part of everyday activity, and not something merely ordered from above. I also learned that the time to look at a company's culture and effect necessary change is not when it's in trouble, but when it's doing well.

Following that principle will enable it to do better when times get tougher, as they assuredly are today. The biggest problem, of course, is sustaining change. And that requires the total commitment, support and understanding of the company's board.

25 August 1991

Geoff Whalen

Geoff Whalen is managing director of the Coventry-based Peugeot Talbot Motor Company. His career in the motor industry spans 25 years. He started with a four-year spell at General Motors. He left in 1970 to join British Leyland as a personnel manager before becoming personnel director of Leyland Cars in 1978. In 1980, he joined what was then the loss-making Peugeot Talbot Motor Company as personnel and industrial relations manager. A year later, he was made assistant managing director. In 1987, after three years as MD, he turned the company into profit.

My biggest mistake was in believing that what I call institutionalized industrial democracy could work at British Leyland.

I went there in 1970 as personnel manager of the Cowley assembly plant after seven years at the National Coal Board in Scotland as a management trainee. I saw the job at BL as a great challenge for I had gained a lot of experience in the Scottish coalfield in dealing with unions. But I quickly found out that industrial relations at BL were in a dismal state. A combination of management paternalism and militant trade unionism had created chaos. The shop stewards' committee was dominated by communists and Trotskyists who competed with one another in extremism. On average, there were two strikes or stoppages each day. But with time we began to put things right.

In 1975, however, when BL got into dire financial straits, it was taken over by the state. As part of the price for restructuring the company, we had to introduce industrial democracy.

The workers' representatives were to be given the right to meet management at plant and board level to discuss and agree business plans. I thought the experiment had a chance of success. But, while consultation is one thing, there is a clear distinction between consultation and what we were told to introduce at BL.

Three things caused the approach to fail. First, shop stewards were neither committed to nor in a position to properly assess the plans they were asked to put their names to.

Second, the workers were reluctant to see their representatives do a management job. Workers thought their union representatives should represent them and leave the running of the plants to management.

Third, BL was subject to all kinds of industrial relations difficulties. There were immense pay problems caused by a crazy pay structure. Moreover, our people had seen little evidence that strikes didn't pay. Only lost wages and lost jobs seemed to bring a sense of reality to industrial relations. In the 1970s, people just did not realize that to survive and prosper, BL needed to improve in almost everything it did.

But I have to say that, in many respects, the industry deserved the poor industrial relations it suffered.

Workers were often treated unfairly. While you don't get results by just being nice, you have to treat people fairly and properly. I've always believed in fair play and in consultation.

In 1974, I chaired the Harmonization Committee at BL to identify and narrow the status differences between white-collar staff and the factory workers. What I learned at BL was put to good effect at Peugeot, where for the past two years everybody has had the same holiday entitlement and the same pension plan – and everybody eats in the same canteen.

We've achieved an enormous improvement in our industrial relations, in productivity, and in quality. We have steady production and we are profitable.

We have a well-established consultation process. Our managers meet regularly with shop stewards, as I do myself, to discuss all matters.

We recognize that we have different roles but a common interest in improving our performance. If we are not competitive and profitable, the efforts to eradicate the injustices of the past will have been wasted.

6 October 1991

Michael Chadwick

Michael Chadwick, 36, is managing director of Chase de Vere Investments. He started his career in 1975 with the merchant bank Manufacturers Hanover. Two years later he trained as an insurance and investment broker with FPC, and became a branch manager in 1980. He was one of the founding directors of Chase de Vere in 1981, and became joint managing director with partner Mike Edge when the company went public three years later. Since 1988, he has run the business on his own. Initially, he found his managers did not have sufficient experience.

My biggest mistake was not having sufficient confidence to delegate. Mike and I were never autocratic, but we did tend to protect people from responsibility. We wanted to ensure they performed to the best of their ability with the minimum of distraction.

It was quite a burden in terms of overall responsibility, but at that stage of the company's growth it was reasonably easy to cope with.

It had always been our intention to delegate, but as the company grew and the pressures increased, we felt even more reluctant to forgo control. Another reason was that the next level of management down involved eight or nine people, all of similar experience but with differing levels of capability, and we wanted to avoid disharmony by promoting some people at the expense of others.

Anyway, all was fine until Mike Edge became ill in 1988. And the problem with a serious illness is that you rarely know how long it's going to take to recover.

When he was first off, it was a question of a week or a month. Nobody ever dreamed it would be three years.

In the beginning, I found myself in a very difficult position. I didn't know to what extent I should be making long-term strategic decisions without him. And I didn't have sufficiently experienced managers to assume responsibility.

Right from the start, people were very sympathetic to the predicament, which made it easier for me to come to terms with the problems. They were constantly coming up and asking if there was anything they could do to help. I suppose I was wary of political manoeuvring. I wondered what their objectives were.

But over a period of time we've all adapted to Mike Edge not being here. People gradually proved they were more than capable of performing the functions that we'd held them back from in the past.

I realized we had been selfish in not wanting to get them involved. They were very bright, ambitious people, and they were performing well. We had underestimated their capacity to do more.

We thought that giving them extra work could detract from what they were supposed to be doing. But by not giving them more, we were actually holding them back.

It took me two years to realize that if only we had delegated before, I wouldn't have been in such a disadvantaged position when Mike became ill. And I have realized that the foundations are so strong now that this company runs extremely well even when I'm not here. I believe it's a weakness if a company is too dependent on any one person.

I did end up making promotions, though I'm still sensitive to upsetting people. But experience has taught me that they do adapt and respect decisiveness. We have incredible loyalty within the company. In the last three years only three people have left out of a staff of 60, which is amazing.

And the more responsibility I have delegated, the more they have rewarded me with the performance they have achieved.

I've got people who are now confident enough to come and tell me when they think I'm doing something wrong. It allows me to step back and make a judgement.

We all tend to overestimate our own importance, and that's probably what we were doing the whole time. If we'd delegated earlier, I think the company would be further ahead.

13 October 1991

Chris Swinson

Chris Swinson, 43, is the national managing partner of BDO Binder Hamlyn. He read philosophy and economics at Oxford University before joining Price Waterhouse as an articled clerk in 1970. He left as an audit manager and in 1979 joined BDO Binder Hamlyn, initially as senior manager, technical services. He became national director of professional standards in 1988 and national managing partner the following year. He is chairman of the financial, reporting and auditing group of the Institute of Chartered Accountants. He has written five books.

My biggest mistake was turning up 24 hours early to temporarily replace a financial management team that hadn't yet been removed. In 1978 I was acting as an audit manager of a large company. Audit managers are the shock troops of a firm, ready to be sent at a moment's notice to the latest crisis or investigation.

Until then, I had spent all my career in an accounting firm, and my experience of practical management was insignificant. There were times when I longed for the responsibilities of a practical manager, rather than those of a professional adviser.

One Friday I received a request to go on the following Monday to a company I had not visited before. It was a small subsidiary of a large group. I was told that the group's management had decided to remove the subsidiary's financial management team. My job was to act as its chief accountant for two or three weeks until they were able to introduce a new team.

My instructions were brief and limited, but my purpose seemed clear and I was looking forward to the experience. This seemed to me an exciting challenge, so it was with a sense of anticipation that I set out on the Monday morning.

On arriving at the company I announced myself boldly, but was a little disconcerted to find my visit was not expected. I found myself waiting in reception for rather a long time and conducting a deep investigation of the contents of a coffee machine.

Eventually someone appeared to see me, and introduced himself as the subsidiary's chief accountant. After the initial, somewhat brief, preliminaries, he asked me exactly what I thought I was doing by turning up and announcing myself as the new chief accountant.

Even though in those days I was green in judgement, I could tell that tact and diplomacy were now called for. As carefully as I could, I explained the instructions I had received and suggested that the best move might be for me to leave as soon as possible to sort out the problem.

My suggestion was readily accepted. On returning to my office, during the afternoon the true story slowly became clear. I had arrived in the company's office a day early.

The group's management had intended to announce the changes they had planned during that same Monday afternoon. No one at the subsidiary expected these changes to be made: my arrival was the first confirmation.

Not surprisingly, the group's management was most annoyed that its carefully laid plans for announcing its decisions had been ruined by an inexperienced accountant who had received garbled instructions.

What did I learn from this? First, I learned always to check my instructions, and often to double-check.

I had not talked to the senior financial management team of the chief client group myself. Had I done this, it would have become clear to them that I had been told to arrive on the Monday. Since then I have never trusted relayed messages.

Second, I have learned to be more sensitive to the environment in which I find myself. The damage that was done by my abortive visit would have been mitigated if I had made sure of my ground before I went.

Finally, I have learned the importance of taking great care in dealing with a company's relationship with its people. My visit rendered the group management's objectives more difficult to achieve, and caused unnecessary distress to several people. I was not asked to return.

27 October 1991

Eric Nicoli

Eric Nicoli, 41, is group chief exceutive of United Biscuits. He began his career at Rowntree in 1972 after taking a degree in physics at Kings College, London. In 1980, he joined United Biscuits as senior marketing controller (biscuit division), then spent three years as marketing director before becoming UK business planning director. In 1985, he became managing director of UB Frozen Foods, and the following year of UB Brands. He was appointed to the board of UB Holdings in 1989 and became chief executive of European Operations. He was appointed group chief executive in January.

My biggest mistake started out as an apparently harmless agreement to help a loyal supplier by speaking at one of his institute's special events. The subject was to be of my choice, provided it was relevant to the institute's work, and therein lay the problem. I had, in effect, agreed to speak on something I knew nothing about.

My initial agreement to participate was irreversible as my supplier called to fix a date, offering any time in the next year and a half. At that time I was struggling to be fully committed for a week and a half, so we picked a date that seemed a long way off – and that was the last I thought of it.

As the occasion approached, however, I began to feel uncomfortable. I realized that with zero knowledge of the subject closest to their hearts, I would be unable to command their attention. In desperation, I called a friend at our main promotions company. I needed an imaginative approach and I needed it quickly.

Within twelve hours I was presented with what seemed the perfect solution. Before my ignorance was exposed entirely, my talk would be interrupted by the appearance of a remote-controlled robot, which I would claim was one of many in everyday use in my company's marketing effort. State of the art technology to inspire the members of the institute to further great work in the future. It sounded pretty good to me.

I had been led to expect a large audience, and I was later to learn that having 30 people turn up was indeed a large number for this particular institute's events. Half of them were people I'd brought along for support and protection.

The robot was obviously a good deal more interesting than I had any chance of being, and the audience immediately came to life with identifiable signs of breathing, and even movement, particularly an attractive lady in the front row whom my helper attempted to molest.

Seconds later, steam came out of the robot's ears – a development I had not expected, but which I felt was extremely clever.

It was only when the steam turned black, visibility fell to zero and the heat from the flames could be felt by all that I realized all was not well. I decided to stop speaking when it occurred to me that people might die if we didn't get out. I urged my minders to put the bloody fire out, only to discover that they too had seen fit to escape.

The entire performance, including the fire and the rescue, lasted some twelve minutes. And when the air eventually cleared, I realized my reputation with the institute had probably gone up in smoke with the robot.

The chairman – my loyal supplier – stumbled to the front to thank me on behalf of the institute. The three remaining people applauded loudly before attacking the finger buffet, and that was the end of that.

I was mortified. But I learnt some important lessons.

First, never, ever, agree to speak publicly about something you know nothing about.

Second, never allow a crisis to develop by leaving preparation to the last minute.

Third, never work with children, animals or robots.

Fourth, the fact that it wasn't the Birmingham Exhibition Centre and the audience wasn't highly influential was no excuse for not taking the event seriously.

Finally, sometimes it's very important to say No.

3 November 1991

Carl Snitcher

Carl Snitcher, 50, is chief executive of the £24m-turnover Paul Raymond Organisation, which has interests in clubs, theatres, publishing and property. He qualified as a lawyer at the University of Cape Town before moving to Britain in 1966. At first he worked for a firm of solicitors in the City, then became the legal officer at Equity, the actors' union, where he stayed for ten years, eventually becoming assistant general secretary, responsible for mechanical media matters. He left the union in 1977, to become chief executive of the Paul Raymond Organisation.

My biggest mistake was name-dropping in order to impress my friends. It made me look an absolute fool.

In the early 1970s, Edward Heath's government was proposing to ban the closed shop and Equity was trying to negotiate an exemption. Our campaign was being masterminded by Gerald Croasdell, the union's general secretary at that time, who decided we should enlist the help of Lord Olivier.

He had recently been ennobled and hadn't yet made a speech in the House of Lords. We knew he was very well disposed towards Equity, so we approached him to see whether he'd be prepared to speak on our behalf. Gerald spoke to him on a Friday afternoon, then asked me to ring him as well to explain a bit about what was required.

I'd never met the man, so I didn't know him at all. But I rang him at the National Theatre, and he asked me to call him at his home in Brighton the following day when he'd had a chance to find out from other peers what he could and couldn't say.

That Saturday morning, some friends of mine who I hadn't seen for a long time arrived from South Africa. I went to their hotel suite, and while we were having tea I asked if I could use their telephone to make a terribly important call to Lord Olivier.

The five of them sat quietly in the room listening to me, and, of course, they could only hear my side of the conversation. It went something like this:

'Good morning, Lord Olivier, it's Carl Snitcher. If you remember, I spoke to you yesterday afternoon about the industrial ... no, Carl Snitcher. And you said ... Carl, yes, Carl Snitcher.

'You were going to speak to Lord ... no, with a 'C'. Carl. You were going to ... Snitcher. S-N-I-T-C- ...'

By this time, people were just falling about on the floor. Here was I, trying to get through to this great man who obviously didn't know who the hell I was, and they thought I was an absolute twit.

He didn't understand what I was talking about, and I came to the conclusion I must have woken him up. My friends were just wetting themselves. I've never seen people laugh as much, and I was mortally embarrassed.

On the Monday, my colleagues and I had to go and see him at the theatre. I was actually scared at the prospect. We walked into his office, and he was sitting with his feet up on the desk, wearing a brace. When Gerald introduced me, Olivier just said: 'You know, I did a film in Hollywood in the Thirties. It was the worst experience of my life. The director's name was Snitcher ... Schneider ... Schitzer or something. He was a shit.'

And that was it. No further conversation was directed at me, though I did try to butt in from time to time. Maybe he thought I was something to do with this horrible director. In the end, he made his speech and we got our exemption. But the point is, there was I, from South Africa, trying to impress my friends with all these terribly important people that I knew, and, the truth was, it just didn't work.

The story of Carl Snitcher, mate of the great, has been told many times since. It was one of the most humiliating experiences of my life. I learnt from that mistake that you have got to be honest about who you do and do not know. You get found out if you overstate your connections, and I have never name-dropped since.

1 December 1991

Peter Davies

Major-General Peter Davies, CB, 53, is chief executive of the Royal Society for the Prevention of Cruelty to Animals. He was educated at Llandovery College, Welbeck College and the Royal Military Academy Sandhurst. He was commissioned into the Royal Signals in 1958, commanded 1st Armoured Division Headquarters and in 1986 was appointed Colonel of the King's Regiment. He served with Royal Air Force, Royal Marines and United Nations troops, and was Commander Communications BAOR prior to becoming GOC Wales. He retired from the Army in November.

My biggest mistake, or certainly the one from which I learnt most, took place in 1962 when I was carrying out an exercise in North Africa which involved a very large deployment of British troops.

I was then a Communications Captain, based at RAF El Adam, and responsible for passing communications from my divisional staff to the two brigades in the desert.

One afternoon we developed a communication fault with one of the brigades and no messages could be passed. Many of the messages were classified. In those days, they had to be translated into code and transmitted to the other end, where another officer would decode them. It was a long and laborious process.

Over a period of eight hours the stack of coded messages built up until shortly before midnight I decided that the only sensible thing to do was to parcel them up and send them by despatch rider, together with an escort, into the desert.

I gave the order for the messages to be bagged – there must have been about 60 – and went off to bed for what I thought was a well-earned rest. At 2am I was woken by a soldier who said the Commanding Officer wanted to see me immediately. Cursing, I got dressed into uniform and moved at reasonably good speed back to my communications centre, where I found him pacing up and down with smoke coming out of his ears.

'Do you not realize what you were doing?' he bellowed. 'Somewhere down in the desert there is a poor man sitting in a trench, getting message after message, which, by hurricane lamp, he has to decode using his books. 'It is going to take him the best part of the next eight hours, during which time the brigade will be moving and he will get cut off again.'

I was pretty inexperienced, but it suddenly dawned on me that I should have destroyed the coded messages and sent the originals in plain English to the brigade, as I had made adequate security provision by ordering an armed escort for them.

The Commanding Officer told me to get into my Land-Rover, take the original messages, and deliver them myself. I drove through the night and, when I eventually arrived, the communications officer was literally up to his ears in these wretched coded messages. He was deciphering as fast as he could, cursing and sweating, with his eyes not quite rolling in his head but as near as dammit. The staff grabbed each message as he finished it to find out what on earth they were supposed to be doing.

Here was a man who had been out on exercise for seven or eight days – moving constantly in the desert, eating not particularly well – and who was very dirty, not having had a bath. He was trying to support his Brigade Commander and staff, and was having a very difficult time of it. What I had done was to add to his troubles and make him look inefficient. He was shattered.

In this case, by the time my brother officer had decoded all the messages most of them would have been worthless, whereas, with a little foresight, I could have saved him a lot of time and trouble.

I just hadn't thought, and, as a result, an officer in arduous conditions was given an almost impossible load which might have broken him. The lesson it taught me – and it is one I have never forgotten – is that whatever order you give to your subordinates, you have to visualize the effect that it is going to have.

26 January 1992

Michael Wade

Michael Wade, 37, is chairman and chief executive of Holman Wade Insurance Brokers, which owns five broking firms: Holman Wade – specializing in insurance for members of Lloyd's – Holman Wade International, Holman Wade Reinsurance Brokers, Hamilton Barr Insurance Brokers and Adam Brothers Contingency. The original Holman Wade was formed in 1980, though today the group is owned by Horace Clarkson plc, of which Michael Wade is an executive director. He was a member of the Task Force looking into the future of the Lloyd's market.

My biggest mistake was failing to realize that a team is no stronger than the weakest link. In 1990 I had targeted another company to acquire. After long and complex negotiations, we decided the only way to crack it was for both boards of directors to meet in one office with our respective lawyers until a deal was completed.

We met on a Tuesday, and by the end of the day we still hadn't reached an agreement. The haggles and the pressures and the egos were unbelievable. There were about fifteen people going off into little huddles, as one side made a demand and the other said: 'Hang on, we'll have to talk about this.' It turned into a complete farce.

We met again on the Wednesday, and all day long we continued to disagree. I was getting quite aggressive and saying: 'Well, this is the way it's going to be, or the deal is off.' Everyone said I was being unreasonable, and by 2am we were all exhausted, so we decided to meet again the following day.

On Thursday morning at 9am I said to my advisers: 'We're going to do this deal today. We're going to insist they agree to our points, and they will, because we've got them over the barrel. We're so nearly there, they can't not do this deal.' And we worded a Stock Exchange announcement to be released once the deal was done.

Meanwhile, we rang the other side to ask whether it was convenient to meet at 11am, or whether to make it an hour later. We agreed to meet at noon. Then, just as I put the phone down, our financial advisers rang and said: 'Congratulations, Michael.'

I said: 'Steady on . . . that's a bit premature.' They said: 'What do you mean, premature?' So I said: 'Well, we're just about to go and do it now.' And they said: 'No, it's flashed up on the Stock Exchange. You've done a deal.'

There was a flurry of activity, and then I discovered that in error the announcement had already been released. Of course, as a public group, we have certain rules and regulations to comply with. My colleagues were ringing up saying the deal had to be struck immediately, otherwise we might come in for criticism from the Stock Exchange and have to withdraw altogether.

To make matters worse, if the other side had known it was already public information, they would have had us over a barrel, and we would have had to have given way on all the points. So I called and said: 'Come straight to the offices. I want to bring the meeting forward by an hour. Don't stop to do anything (certainly don't open your newspapers or switch the television on or take any calls), it's imperative that you come now.' For the third day running we all met with our lawyers. I said: 'Hi everybody, I'm Mr Reasonable this morning,' and suddenly I was charm personified, giving way on points I had been fighting over for weeks. They couldn't work out what on earth was going on, and were so astonished that, of course, we signed the deal.

Until this day, they never knew what had happened. But the lesson to be learnt is that in any deal situation, you have to take great care within the grand plan never to forget the detail, because a relatively small clerical mistake can cause the most massive problem if you don't spot it. Releasing that announcement prematurely was a big mistake, but one which, happily, we managed to get around. And I don't think it will ever happen again.

1 March 1992

John Garnett

John Garnett CBE, 70, was the director of the Industrial Society from 1962 until his retirement in 1986. He then spent four years as chairman of West Lambeth Health Authority, and now works principally for the Post Office, improving leadership skills on all levels. After naval service during the Second World War he spent fifteen years at ICI, where he became the first head of communication. He was a member of the Wilberforce Court of Enquiry which looked into the miners' dispute in 1971 and was the arbitrator of the lorry drivers' strike in 1977.

My biggest mistake was trying to sell ideas in relation to my own objectives, rather than the objectives of the people I was selling to. At 12.45pm on 15 December 1959 I was called from my office, where I was the personnel manager of the plastics division of ICI, to see the chairman.

He informed me that after working for three years at the plastics division, where we had achieved some great things which are now in the history books of ICI, I was required to leave and go back to head office.

My work, in the view of the board, was irrelevant and, more seriously, distracting. They were in the business of making profits in plastics, while I seemed to be in the business of developing people, which took their eyes off the main purpose.

At the age of 41, with my fourth child born only three weeks before, it was, of course, a shattering experience. I went back to head office and got my career going again, but it took at least a year to recover from the blow. All the time I wondered what had gone wrong, and why did it happen to me? Gradually it dawned on me that it was all my own fault.

I have always felt passionately about the development of people. I had joined ICI as a clerk and worked my way up, but the terrible thing about industry in those days was that you could have all kinds of talents, enthusiasm and ideas, and nobody seemed to want them.

If you worked 20 minutes late, they used to say: 'Haven't you got a home to go to?' But that wasn't the way I was brought up. If there was a job to do, you carried on working until it was done.

ICI cared enormously about the welfare of its employees, but that wasn't enough. People long to know what is going on, and how they can contribute. That's what makes life exciting, but there was none of that at ICI. And I was determined as I rose up in the company to do something about it. In fact, that's what I dedicated the rest of my life to: getting people going, calling forth their gifts.

During the three years I spent with the plastics division we had introduced staff assessment, job evaluation and team briefing . . . a whole mass of things. We got the management to communicate with employees, used union representatives to find out what employees thought, and so on. We made immense changes which are now standard procedure, but in trying to get people excited about these ideas, it never occurred to me to make them relevant to their purposes.

I had totally failed when speaking to the board or my colleagues in management to start by saying 'We, of course, are in the business of making profits in plastics. In order to do that, we must really call forth and use the gifts of our people, because they are the greatest resource we have.' Because I failed to make that point, I lost my job. But I never made that mistake again.

Two years later, I was asked to become the director of the Industrial Society. When I first joined we earned £165,000 a year; 24 years later we had a staff of 350 and earned £10m a year. Whenever we wanted a company to use our ideas, I insisted that our staff find out first from the chief executive what his objectives were. Our practical suggestions for getting the best out of people could help him achieve them, but they had to be sold on that basis.

8 March 1992

Clive Jenkins

Clive Jenkins, 65, is general secretary emeritus of Manufacturing Science and Finance, the largest skills union in the world. He joined a metallurgical test house at fourteen and was Britain's youngest ever full-time trade union official at 21. He was general secretary of the Association of Scientific, Technical and Managerial Staffs from 1970 to 1988 – the radical white-collar union of which he was also founder – and secretary of the ASTMS parliamentary committee. From 1987 to 1988 he was president of the Trades Union Congress before he became joint general secretary of the MSF.

I am not arrogant, but I have been influenced by the leader who once declared: 'I have only made one mistake. Briefly, 20 years ago, I thought I was wrong on an important issue . . . but I was only wrong about my being wrong.'

In my professional life, I rather narcissistically still take that view. But if I ever did make anything resembling a mistake, it was in getting Norman Tebbit his very first broadcast.

In the early 1970s, at the time of Edward Heath's attempts to intrude into trade unions, I was telephoned by Andrew Boyle, author of *The Fourth Man* and significant biographies of leading figures, who was then producing The World At One. I was appearing on the programme regularly, and Andrew said to me: 'We want someone to oppose you, and we're looking for a fresh face.'

I was then very actively involved in bargaining on behalf of airline staff, and I had heard of a pilot, called Norman Tebbit, in what was then the British Overseas Airways Corporation. He was a firebrand, they said. A very active leader. Norman had just become the MP for Epping. In fact, I think he was the prototype for Essex Man.

So I suggested him to Andrew, who invited Norman to take part in the debate. On the day, his demeanour was ashen. He had never made a broadcast before, and as we sat together, facing William Hardcastle, his fingers drummed on the table, which, of course, was like an earthquake to the sensitive BBC microphone. So I put my little hand over his, and restrained him.

Afterwards, Bill Hardcastle remarked that it was very professional of me. I didn't ever put my hand over Norman's again, though in time we got to know each other quite well. You may not believe this, but when he's not in his professional confrontational pose, he's really quite funny.

Many years later, when Norman was secretary of state for employment, the educational grant for the TUC's programme came under threat. So, as chairman of the educational committee, I went with the secretary to see him. There was only one other person in the meeting; a young woman in knee-length socks.

In that meeting, Norman said to me: 'Why should I give you money to train Bolshevik shop stewards?' I patiently explained that we were seeking to train people to be sensitive, and to avoid accidental confrontations – and in the end we kept our grant. I even believe that I once saw Norman in a picket line when some pilots were being dismissed, but he denied it unequivocally when I put it to him a few years ago at an embassy reception.

But my regret is that I had no way of foreseeing, when I put his name forward for that broadcast, that this BOAC pilot would become a part of the gang which later harassed the Labour party in the House of Commons and ensured Margaret Thatcher's election.

If there is a moral, it is the dictum that senior counsel has in court: never ask a witness a question if you don't know what the answer is going to be.

So, to turn that around, never recommend someone for a position, particularly for a first broadcast – an illumination of a political personality – unless you know where it's going to lead. And that was my mistake. I didn't know what he was going to turn into. Of course, I don't think he did either.

26 April 1992

Sir George Turnbull

Sir George Turnbull was born in 1926 and read mechanical engineering at Birmingham University. In 1950 his career in the automotive industry began with Standard Motors. By 1962 he was director and general manager of Standard-Triumph International, which was taken over by British Leyland in 1968. Sir George became managing director of British Leyland in 1973. From 1974 he worked overseas with foreign automotive manufacturers, returning to the UK in 1979 as chairman of Talbot. In 1984, he joined Inchcape, becoming chairman and chief executive in 1986. He is chairman of the Industrial Society's council and executive of the International Chamber of Commerce.

With hindsight, the biggest mistake in my business career was not delegating authority to those around me in my early years. Nowadays, I am a great delegator and it is easy because I have such good people around me at Inchcape. But back in the 1960s, as a young executive in the British motor industry, my management style was very different.

It was not until the merger of the Leyland group with British Motor Corporation in 1968 that I learnt my lesson. For the six years before that I was general manager of Standard-Triumph, which was part of the Leyland group and best known for producing the TR series and Spitfire sports cars. It was a business employing about 17,000 people around the world and I used to run it in a very hands-on fashion. I would not say I was autocratic, but I really did impress my personality on the organization. I expected to be consulted on big issues and all the major decisions had to come to me. Looking back, I did not allow the managers underneath me as much freedom to manage as I should have done.

One result of this hands-on approach was that with some of my managers I mistook loyalty for ability and did not look outside the business for the best people.

Perhaps with hindsight if I had brought in a little more expertise at Triumph, and delegated more to my existing management team, it might well have survived the rationalization programme which followed. A lot of things might have been different if I had been more perceptive about the skills needed in some parts of the group.

I saw the light after the merger of Leyland and BMC in 1968. The merger was orchestrated by the Labour Government with the aim of ensuring a strong British presence in the international motor industry. I became deputy managing director of the combined group under Lord Stokes and also managing director of BL Austin Morris, the volume car side of the business. It was then that I realized I had to delegate and I could not run the business without some very high-quality lieutenants around me. I began to realize how much more I could leave people to do on their own, and we also recruited heavily from the other big car companies, including Ford. I think the penny would have dropped eventually anyway. But it was only when I got to Longbridge in 1968 that I realized I could not afford the luxury or the time of trying to do everything myself. I had to delegate and it led to much better business decisions. Longbridge forced me to look at management in a much more modern and innovative way.

Before I went on to Longbridge I had always tended to promote people from within and never looked outside or used executive search agencies. Again, that was undoubtedly my mistake. It was my arrogance to think I could do it without any outside recruitment and do everything from inside.

Now I am a convert to using executive search agencies for any key executive post. At the end of the day, the best managers are the ones who collect the best professionally qualified people around them and get them to work together.

1 April 1990

Part Three

Financial Mistakes

In a sense, all the mistakes collected in this book are financial. This is because business – whatever its role in the community and other activities – is still essentially about making money, and if a mistake hits the business it will diminish its ability to make money.

But those in this particular section have money or finances at their heart rather than as an effect.

Some are clear examples of the lack of experience that is typical in the small organization founded by an entrepreneur. For instance, David Bruce, founder of the Firkin pubs, describes himself as a victim of his own success. Having failed maths O-Level five times, he – like many others – did not understand that cash is not the same as profit. Fooled by the ringing tills into thinking that he was succeeding, he did not bother himself unduly with the paperwork and nor did he – until it was almost too late – appoint a finance director to take care of that side of the business. It all ended happily enough, but it could easily have gone the other way.

Likewise, sales promotion specialist Alan Toop says his mistake was to start up in business without realizing the importance of cash flow. Although this is basic stuff to an accountant, it is not uppermost in the mind of somebody keen to become their own boss. And part of Mr Toop's problem was that he had previously worked for large organizations, where 'cash was something you obtained by simply turning on a tap once your profit-and-loss budgets had been approved by the board'. Fortunately for him, he belatedly realized that the original finance for the company was running out rather quickly, and – largely through paying particular attention to invoices – he was able to save the situation. But his company nearly collapsed within months of its foundation – as do many.

Luxury lingerie retailer Janet Reger, for instance. Encouraged by a strong start, Ms Reger took on what turned out to be too many financial commitments. The result was that when the downturn came she could not service her debts. Liquidation was the only answer.

But sophisticated, experienced businessmen can make financial mistakes. Swraj Paul of Caparo, for instance, is the man who sought redress for the loss he had incurred in taking over a company that was not as profitable as its accounts suggested. He lost his suit, but the case and the issues it raised have become part of the background to the continuing debate over the role of auditors.

On the other hand, Terry Maher, who has made is name for his attacks on the net book agreement, says his mistake when purchasing a company was to be persuaded to use a formula now known as an earn-out deal. Basically a way of bridging the difference between the price the seller seeks and that the purchaser is prepared to pay, it involves making a small initial payment and linking the rest to future profits. Which is fine if all goes well, but more complicated if – as happened in 1980 – a recession intervenes. Mr Maher does not regret the deal, just the method of payment. But as he says, 'small things can turn into major problems'.

It is perhaps surprising that experienced business people can fall foul of share deals. But no fewer than three of the contributions to this section involve that kind of mistake. All three display a philosophical attitude now, but their errors must have seemed catastrophic at the time.

Incidentally, one of them – the former Conservative MP Anthony Beaumont-Dark who was invited to contribute because of his work in the investment business – provides another example of something looking like a mistake but then appearing a wise move. 'One of the worst things I have done is choosing right and selling early,' he says. 'Polly Peck was a classic case. I invested about £1,100 and within months had made about £9,000 and sold the shares. But if I still had them now they would be worth about three-quarters of a million.' Not long after he said that the shares were worthless.

At the time of going to press, we were still to find out whether George Walker had learned from his mistake. His experience in the early 1980s of having to guarantee personally a loan he needed in order to carry out a deal he did not want to do had convinced him that he would never again stake his home and family against a business, he said.

Since then, though, he has lost his position at the helm of Brent Walker as part of the price of the company's restructuring. And, although his personal position was not apparently affected, there were doubts over his future.

George Walker

George Walker, 61, became a professional boxer after he left school. Using his winnings and those of his brother Billy, he started a fast food chain and operated taxis, long-distance lorries and petrol stations. He built up a business developing property and gained a stock market quotation in 1974. In 1982 he took his company private to avoid being taken over, coming back to market in 1985. Today Brent Walker turns over £526m in leisure and brewing.

My biggest mistake was staking my home life against my business life and nearly losing both. In 1982, I was chief executive of Brent Walker, the public company it had taken me 20 years to build. Mike Luckwell of The Moving Picture Company bought 5 per cent of the company and came to see me and my directors to try to buy our shares, and then bid for the company. I didn't want to sell the business, but a couple of the directors wanted to. They were good friends of mine, and the only way I could oppose that was to say, 'I'll buy your shares instead.' That took my shareholding above the limit, to 33 per cent, and even though I didn't have the money, the Stock Exchange said I had to bid for the lot and take the company private. This was at a time when the economy was in similar shape to today, and I found it very, very difficult to borrow the money. Eventually I borrowed £2.75m from a small independent bank in Brighton called TCB, at an interest rate of 4 per cent over Libor. I guaranteed the loan personally, putting up all my properties, including my home, against it. My wife Jean, who has always worked in the business with me, also had to sign. If the company went down, we would be penniless.

My first move was to sell Oxford Walk, a shopping development in Oxford Street which was costing us a lot and making a loss. I thought it would take three months to sell, but some of the shopkeepers tried to hold on to their leases by taking me to court, and it took eighteen months instead. That was a real setback.

So we sold the cinemas and worked the business nearly to death. We cut back on staff, sold the company cars and sold properties that weren't producing a good cash-flow or profit. There was one three-month period that I didn't even make enough money to pay the company's interest, never mind my own, which was over 19 per cent. I had to go round clearing the tills on a Thursday night so I could pay my staff on the Friday. It was a year-and-a-half of hell. I couldn't sleep and I was living on Mogadon. I used to sit up at night in my darkest moments and wonder if I would lose everything. Jean and I had started married life 20 years ago with very little, now we had a good life. How would I tell my children that we had lost everything?

We had invested what was for the company at that time a considerable sum of money in making a Gilbert and Sullivan film series. They were given bad reviews and we'd had no great hopes for them. But suddenly they took off like a steam train, all around the world. They're still selling on video today.

Then, in 1985 the Brighton Marina project came up. We needed to raise £13m within six months to buy it, and I decided to take the company public again. The flotation raised a net £7.75m and I borrowed the outstanding £5m as a further personal loan.

We got the Marina and obtained planning permission for a superstore. That was sold for £10m, which allowed me to pay off the debts, including my £5m loan, and have a couple of million to spare. After all that I ended up with a huge gastric ulcer that burst and had to be operated on. But I was back at work in ten days, and I was able to sell some of my shares in the company to pay back the £2.75m, leaving me with 26 per cent of the company. The Marina was the perfect end to an horrendous three years. At times I had even had to beg and borrow from friends and relatives to pay my interest off – they were very good to me. All through that time I really thought I had made the biggest mistake of my life, the pressure was so intense. At the end of it I realized that the real mistake was subjecting my wife and family to that. I would never again stake my home and family against a business. If I want to put my neck on the block or commit business suicide, that's fine, but I won't drag my wife and family down with me.

3 June 1991

Anthony Beaumont-Dark

Anthony Beaumont-Dark, 57, has been Conservative MP for Birmingham Selly Oak since 1979. After attending Birmingham College of Arts and Crafts and Birmingham University, he trained as an investment analyst. He has been a director of several companies and is a consultant for Smith Keen Cutler, where he was senior partner for twelve years. A member of the House of Commons Treasury and Civil Service Select Committee, he is a governor of Aston and Birmingham universities.

In the investment business we are a bit like fishermen. It's the good ones that get away that most get you. And while I have had plenty of successes, I have had many that have got away.

One of the worst things I have done is choosing right and selling early. Polly Peck was a classic case. I invested about £1,100 and within months had made about £9,000 and sold the shares. But if I still had them now they would be worth about three-quarters of a million. It makes an idiocy of the first Lord Rothschild's remark that you make your money by always selling early.

There have also been cases when I have bought when I should have sold. Too often you reinforce failure and sell success. You tend to think that if shares were right at 75p they are bound to be better at 50p. But you shouldn't reinforce failure. Rather, you should admit failure and reinforce success.

That's true of professionals as well as amateurs. Obviously, when something like Black Monday happens the good, the bad and the ugly all fall together. But the good, the bad and the ugly often go up together. It sounds simple, but it's the devil's own job to keep reminding yourself of that. I remember being told when I started in the business that I might think that I was awfully good, but I had to remember that I had just joined at a good time for the market.

For instance, I got stuck with Eagle Trust. I was very fond of a company called Mitchell Somers. There was a merger and it became part of Eagle Trust and I thought it was going to be fantastic. But I had forgotten that the fundamentals had changed. In this, £60,000 became I don't know what. I've written it off.

Also, back in 1973–4, when – with rising oil prices and the like – it looked as if the world was going to end, I bought lots of gold and baked beans. I've eaten the baked beans, but I am stuck with about £30,000-worth of gold to this day. I'm not losing money, but if you take inflation into account I haven't done very well. But then if the big bad day does come I'll be all right.

There are a number of other important rules in investment – particularly, as long as you never invest more than you are willing to lose you cannot come to any harm. Don't think about the amount you want to make – that is limitless. But be clear about how much you are prepared to lose. As I said when I was asked how much I had lost on Black Monday, 'I've lost too much to laugh about and not enough to cry about.'

Allied to this is another old adage about never putting all your eggs in one basket – and I always think of this when I hear of people losing everything in affairs like the Dunsdale collapse. Never put all your eggs in one basket because – no matter how good it appears – you never know how good the basket is going to be.

However, the great thing I have learned about the business is how you can sell short on shares.

I sold short on what was then Anglo-Iranian and became BP. This was about 30 years ago and I was in my twenties. A person I had huge respect for told me to sell Anglo-Iranian, and I sold my 100 shares and 400 I hadn't got. If I have ever lain awake at night it was then. I had to buy the 400 shares back at a £1,100 loss, which was a lot of money 30 years ago.

I am naturally quite a cheerful person, but I felt distinctly gloomy for quite a long time. I once stared at myself in the mirror and realized I could have been broke. I had just about got the money, so I was all right, but that was the most scary thing I ever did. It taught me to never do anything so foolish as to put myself in a limitless debt situation, and ever since I have never sold short.

Nor have I have ever bought anything apart from my house on credit – because you are never master of your destiny when you're in debt.

24 June 1990

Terry Maher

Terry Maher has become a controversial figure in publishing circles for his attack on the net book agreement, through Dillons bookstores. Trained as a chartered accountant, he purchased Pentos as a £100 off-the-shelf company in 1972. He took it public by reversing into Cape Town & District Gaslight & Coke Co. The company then underwent rapid expansion building up interests from engineering to publishing. Hit hard by the recession, Pentos concentrated on its core companies – Dillons, Athena, Ryman and Caplan.

The mistakes I have made in business have nearly always been when I have failed to follow my instincts. In 1978 I made the mistake of purchasing a company using a formula which has become popular over recent years. Today that kind of deal is called an earn-out, but at that time the term hadn't been coined. I was uneasy, although I allowed myself to be persuaded into it.

Earn-outs are a deceptively attractive way of bridging the difference between the asking price and the price the purchaser thinks a company is worth. You pay a small initial payment and the rest is calculated as a multiple, not an historic profit but as the future profit. It all seems incredibly reasonable.

Naturally there have to be safeguards to protect the seller against interference, otherwise an unscrupulous purchaser might starve the company of cash and resources, push profits down to depress the final price and then expand.

It is usual to draw up an agreement which sets out a number of conditions covering capital expenditure, marketing expenditure and so on. These can be changed only by mutual agreement. As long as the world continues as it is, there is no conflict. But things can change very fast. The problem with such agreements is that responsibility rests with the owners but control does not. People have different views on risk. But the owner in effect has his hands tied. To protect his interests he may need to act, but if he does he might be in breach of the agreement of non-interference. In addition these agreements can lead to an unhealthy obsession with short-term performance. Despite my misgivings, in 1978 we purchased Gardencast, a small but successful company selling cast-aluminium garden furniture, which we believed would complement our aluminium greenhouse company, Halls. It was thought then that their sales objectives could be easily met because of our ability to help with sales to the major High Street chains. Purchase price was to be based on profits in 1978, 1979 and 1980.

What actually happened was that at the beginning of 1980 we entered a major recession in UK manufacturing industry, with very high interest rates and a dramatic reduction in consumer demand – conditions which make the present mini-recession seem very small beer. High Street retailers destocked rapidly; orders were cut by more than 50 per cent, which was far more than anybody had envisaged. There was a need to act quickly to reduce capacity and conserve capital.

We decided to reduce overheads by merging administrative departments. External warehousing was closed and consolidated within Halls' existing facilities. A further priority was to reduce excessive stockholding by cutting orders from the Czech supplier. In these circumstances there was inevitable conflict as to who was responsible for trading profits turning into losses. For instance it was possible to argue that a merged sales force was less effective in selling Gardencast furniture and that sales had fallen because the range had been reduced. It eventually led to litigation on their part. We settled because by our act of taking control, a case could be made that we had been in breach of the original agreement.

Taking control was not the mistake; the mistake was entering that kind of agreement in the first place. The reason I did so was that it was a small company and one which we felt would fit well, but small things can turn into major problems if they go wrong and in this instance we lost £½ m, which was a large sum at the time.

15 July 1990

Lord Young

Lord Young of Graffham, 58, trained and worked as a solicitor before going into business. Following the 1979 general election, he went into public service, becoming chairman of the Manpower Services Commission in 1982. In 1984, he joined the Cabinet, going on to serve as Employment Secretary and Trade and Industry Secretary. He subsequently became executive chairman of Cable & Wireless. His memoirs of his time in government, *The Enterprise Years*, were published in 1990.

My biggest mistake occurred back in the 1970s. In the previous decade I had built up a company called Eldonwall, which used to build industrial estates beside the new motorways and was involved in various types of contracting. In 1970, I sold out to Town & City Properties, then the third-largest property company in the country, and a few months later I joined the board. I worked there in 1971–2. But at Christmas 1972 I had a disagreement with Barry East, the head of the company, over the direction it should take, and became non-executive.

The next year was the most depressing year of my life. I thought that I had enough money – more would only spoil my children – and I considered going back to university. Richard Marsh, chairman of British Rail then, asked me to take over the running of the British Rail Property Board, but at the last minute I withdrew.

I had been very friendly with Jeffrey Sterling, now Sir Jeffrey and head of P & O, for many years and we had done a number of deals together, including developing Earls Court and Olympia. He suggested that we look at the redevelopment of exhibition centres around the world, so we arranged to go to Singapore, Japan and the Philippines, flying out on a Monday morning in October 1973.

I was the director with the second-largest shareholding in Town & City after Barry East, and on that day my broker phoned to say that shares in the company were then trading at 116p and were going to be 125p by Christmas. I asked him to sell a few hundred thousand shares at 125p – I had done a quick calculation that it would be enough to pay off all my borrowings. But as soon as I had put the phone down I thought, 'That's being too greedy. I should really sell now.' And that's the mistake I made.

I tried to phone him back before I left the office, but he was not there. I tried to call him again from the airport departure lounge – again he was not there. This was before the days of carphones. I began to have an uneasy feeling.

We got on the plane and during the long flight – after I had finished reading what I had to read and played a game of chess with Jeffrey – I got out a piece of paper and worked out my assets, mainly shares in Town & City, and my liabilities, bank borrowings. I found that my liabilities were just 8 per cent of my assets.

But by the time we landed in the Far East we had flown through Black Tuesday and the price of Town & City had dropped to 90p – there was no way I could sell the shares.

By the time I came back to England, they were in the 70s. At the time I thought of joining a syndicate to buy the shares and try to stabilize the price. Fortunately, we didn't because by February the price was down to 3¾ p.

There is a good side to everything, however. All my depression went away and I decided that I had to go out and earn my living again. I sold all my shares at 3¾ p and started again. I've been lucky enough to be able to do it twice.

I began in 1974–5 with a joint venture with Manufacturers Hanover. I did that for five or six years and then decided to take a two-year holiday and go into government. In fact, it lasted for ten years. I did that because I had got so fed up with the way the country had been run and was very impressed with what Mrs Thatcher was doing. I had not done national service, so I saw this as a version of it – without the square-bashing.

25 November 1990

David Bruce

David Bruce, 42, failed his maths 'O' level five times before leaving school to work for a brewery. In 1979, he came off the dole queue to open the Goose and Firkin pub in London after raising a loan against his home. By 1988 he had built a chain of eighteen pubs which he sold for £6.6m, intending to retire with his £2m share. But he could not resist going back into business and is now trading as Inn Securities and building up a chain of Hedgehog and Hogsheads pubs outside London.

My biggest mistake was not paying proper attention to my accounts in the early days of the Firkin pubs. We had opened the Goose and Firkin in London in 1979 and I was working 18 lousy hours a day, seven days a week, brewing the beer in the cellar and surviving on adrenalin. I had eight staff and a part-time bookkeeper.

Everybody said the pub would not work, but people were queueing to get in. It was tremendously exciting and I was on a complete high. The tills were ringing, my break-even point was £2,500 a week but the pub never did less than £4,500.

So why, I thought, if one has created this extraordinary thing, should one scuttle back home to Battersea and spend hours doing boring old paperwork? The turnover was so good I did not even bother with profit and loss accounts. (And you have to bear in mind that I did not have a natural aptitude for figures.)

In May 1980, I opened the Fox and Firkin in Lewisham. I trained a brewer to look after the Goose, but he promptly broke his leg, leaving me to deal with both pubs. There was even less time to do paperwork.

Then I opened another pub in London, and because the experts doomed us to failure I thought it would be easier if the pubs traded under separate companies. Each one had a different accounting year – it was a good lesson in how not to run a business.

By the time we had opened our fourth pub in 1981, our solicitors, Bishop and Sewell, had watched our progress with great interest and assumed we were incurring a hideous tax bill, so they suggested we met with accountants Touche Ross. My wife Louise and I went along with what little financial information we had, plus a couple of audits which showed we had traded at a loss from day one.

In fact, while the turnover for the first year was £1m, we had made losses of £86,000. One of their corporate finance partners said if I did not appoint a chartered accountant to the board as financial director immediately we would go bust within a couple of months. So I took on someone from a major brewery who introduced systems such as stock control and weekly profit-and-loss accounts.

But that did not solve the immediate problems. Touche Ross also said I would have to sell one of the pubs, the Fleece and Firkin in Bristol, because it was costing too much time and money. Reluctantly I put it on the market. By now it was obvious that I should have appointed a finance director at the beginning. The bank was getting nervous, my borrowings were rising and I was not producing a profit.

If the bank had pulled the rug we would have gone down personally for £500,000. Touche Ross advised me to sell a small percentage of the equity, which of course I did not want to do.

Eventually I struck a satisfactory deal with 3i (Investors in Industry) which bought 10 per cent of the business and gave us a loan. Better cash control enabled us to turn a loss into profit, and the following year, on a turnover of £1.6m we showed a profit of £47,000.

Touche Ross, who charged us under £5,000 to sort the problem out, have done my audits ever since. Paul Adams, our managing director, is the resident chartered accountant. He has kept costs down and introduced budgets which the staff can stick to.

In hindsight the solutions were obvious, but I was a victim of my own success. If the turnover had not been so good I would have realized a lot sooner how close I was to bankruptcy.

16 December 1990

Nik Powell

Nik Powell, 40, is co-chairman of the Palace Group. He first made his name as the partner of Richard Branson in Virgin Records. When he finally lost interest in the music industry, he moved into the audio-visual market. In 1981, Mr Powell opened the Video Palace in order to learn about the film business from the retail end. The following year he started up Palace Video, a successful film distribution and production company. He is currently bidding in a consortium for a television franchise.

I wouldn't necessarily describe any mistake as my 'biggest'. But there was one film where we made such a group of interconnected mistakes that the company was severely hurt.

Several years ago we started working on a film which we co-produced with an American doing his first big feature film. Not only that, but we included a clause in the contract under which everything had to be mutually agreed, and that proved to be a fundamental problem during the whole course of production.

Initially we got it financed – and this was another mistake – by an individual who was keen to get into the film business, rather than by someone already in the industry. We had sold the American rights to Lorimar for about half the cost of the movie, so he was discounting that contract and undertook to provide the rest of the production costs.

But once we started shooting, the financier backed out. We found a British company prepared to back us and signed the deal, but then had to pull out because our co-producer would not sign. He still thought the original investor would come up with the money. Eventually the American backer started to do so, but not enough to cover all our costs.

Finally the co-producer asked us to approach Embassy Pictures (now called Nelson). Embassy offered us £1.6m for the rest of the world rights, which covered our basic costs, and we signed. But again the co-producer refused to sign, this time because he thought, like many people making their first film, that it was the greatest movie ever and we were selling it too cheaply.

By now the American financier and Palace were out of pocket by around £2m between us. Fortunately we owned the negative, so when we finished filming I took it back to London and suspended all post-production in order to get the co-producer to negotiate. He did, but it took about two months, during which the interest on all the debts was rolling up and Palace experienced severe financial difficulties as a result.

Eventually we hammered out a deal under which the individual financier took over all the existing debt and repaid Palace the majority of its money. We retained the UK rights because that was the only way to get back the balance.

But much later, just before the picture was due to be released, the financier – at the behest of the co-producer – took out an injunction and challenged the part of the contract which said we had UK rights. The injunction was overturned by us but the delay caused enormous damage to the release.

Meanwhile the co-producer had done the rounds, trying to sell the world rights, and in the end did a deal with another film company, J&M, for £900,000. On a discounted cashflow basis this was only worth £500,000, more than £1m short of the deal Embassy had offered us one and a half years earlier. We could have saved all the pain, the court cases, everything.

Now we are extremely cautious and only do a deal like this if the other people are equally at risk, and we have a clause giving Palace the final say. I learned to be extremely cautious about people investing in films who do not have both financial skills and experience in the feature film business. Never again will we go ahead with projects before the contracts are absolutely tied down.

So it added up to a major mistake, but it also taught me a hell of a lot of lessons. I'm a great believer that failure is a much better teacher than success. And at least we got our money back.

13 January 1991

Swraj Paul

Swraj Paul is the man at the heart of the Caparo/Fidelity/Touche Ross affair after his company purchased another whose accounts subsequently proved fraudulent. Now 60, he has lived in England since 1966 when he brought his younger daughter from India for medical treatment. Tragically she died, but he stayed and has built up Caparo Group. The company owns 80 per cent of the quoted Caparo Industries. A close friend and biographer of the late Indira Ghandi, he founded the Indo-British Association in 1975 and was made Padma Bhushan (equivalent to a British peerage).

My biggest mistake happened during the takeover of Fidelity by my company Caparo, when I relied too much on the verity of published accounts. I was born in India and grew up in the family steel business, training as an engineer. I came to England in 1966 and in 1969 began building up the Caparo Group. We manufactured and traded steel during the late 1970s and early 1980s when metal bashing was very unfashionable.

But by the mid 1980s we wanted to diversify into a sunrise industry. So we thought about going into electronics and decided to take over Fidelity, the hi-fi and radio manufacturer. It was capitalized at about £11m and had reported profits of £1.4m in the year to 1984 and we had picked up from the market that management was weak.

It was a family business, run by the Dickman brothers who held 22 per cent of the shares. We launched a hostile bid in June and acquired the company for £14m in October, keeping the brothers on.

In 1975, after I came to this country and started in business, James Leek joined as my number two. He's a chartered accountant and very proud of his profession.

I remember arguing because I was used to Indian accounts where accountant's statements are longer than chairmen's, but he always assured me that you could trust audited accounts in England. By 1984, having acquired several quoted companies and seen it for myself, I started agreeing with him. So when we took over Fidelity I had no reason to think that the £1.4m profit figure was inaccurate. After all, it had been audited by Touche Ross. Nor, from the defence document Fidelity produced, was there any indication that the profits for 1984–5 would not be as good.

But within two months we came to the conclusion that the company had made a loss in 1983–4.

The first clue came from the factories which seemed to operate on a hand-to-mouth basis. Every day there would be a stoppage because some component had run out. Yet according to the balance sheet we had about £8m of components.

It took quite a bit of time for our managers to go into it. Suppliers and customers were rather coy in response to our questions and it wasn't until we asked the Dickman brothers to leave that the truth gradually emerged. It was terrible. After six months we knew we were looking at a case of fraud. In January this year the court awarded Caparo damages against Steven and Robert Dickman who, it said, had overstated Fidelity's profits by £1.78m in its accounts.

Caparo tried to sue Touche Ross for negligence but the Law Lords ruled that when preparing reports auditors had no duty of care to potential investors. We have now issued another writ against Touche Ross but this time in the name of our subsidiary Fidelity, now called Intersound Consumer Electronics. This writ includes a claim for breach of contract as well as alleging negligence by Touche Ross as Fidelity's auditors.

It has hurt me in two ways. One, of course, was financial. Fidelity was a very big hit for us (we were only capitalized at about £20m) and we really had to struggle to carry it.

The second was the shock. I believed the accounts. It has been a very painful experience – I hate to get into litigation. It put us off contested takeovers for several years.

In sum, I think the new accounting standards will be wonderful and yesterday would not be too soon to bring them in.

19 May 1991

Alan Toop

Alan Toop, 57, is president of The Sales Machine International, a sales promotion consultancy with offices in Britain, Italy and the US. He took a degree in English Literature at University College, London, before joining Unilever, where he worked in marketing for eight years. He then spent two years in advertising with J Walter Thompson before setting up The Sales Machine International, now one of Europe's top sales-promotion companies. Its clients have included Quaker Oats, Courvoisier and Brooke Bond. He has written several books on the subject.

My biggest mistake was to start my own company without having the slightest idea of the importance of cash flow. After working for Unilever and J Walter Thompson, I thought it would be nice to be my own boss.

People were encouraging me to be a sales-promotion specialist. I had already written *Choosing the Right Sales Promotion* and I saw an opportunity to start a business.

The Sales Machine International was set up in 1970 to offer a creative consultancy service in sales promotion.

We got off to a brisk start. Lots of blue-chip companies expressed an interest, and they were soon giving us assignments.

Prospects for the new company seemed bright. We clearly had an early success on our hands; entrepreneurial daring was meeting with its just reward. The budget for year one showed our target income, a detailed analysis of expenditure, and predicted a small profit.

I was good at this sort of budgeting exercise. In the past, I had been required to prepare them for big brands I was responsible for, and I was well trained in controlling them tightly.

Of course, I knew we would need some money to finance the company. I had taken a pot-shot at £10,000 – about £100,000 in today's terms – and I had arranged all that with the bank. After four months, our income was on target and expenditure was as budgeted. Great.

We did, however, seem to be using the £10,000 rather quickly. So, for the first time, I sat down quietly, wrote the next six months across the top of a sheet of paper, and under each month, pencilled in how much money we were due to receive and how much we were due to pay out. I had in fact reinvented the concept of a cash-flow forecast. Reinvented, because in the positions I had held in big corporations, cash was something you obtained by simply turning on a tap once your profit-and-loss budgets had been approved by the board.

What this cash-flow forecast demonstrated was that the cash was going to run out in three months. My biggest mistake was about to prove terminal. The company was going bust.

I was devastated. All this apparent success was crumbling in my hands. For the first time, I realized the total inadequacy of profit-and-loss budgets. In the event, we managed to salvage the company – just. All my time was concentrated on attempting to improve disastrous cash flow.

Terms of business were rewritten, staged invoicing dates were built into all new assignments and hurriedly renegotiated on current projects.

We literally went back to clients and said: 'We would like to send you an interim invoice. And we'd like to do it today. By hand.' I did it myself. It was crucial to the survival of the business.

Overdue invoices were vigorously chased. Cash-flow forecasts became the key management tool of the business, and nothing was more important than updating them monthly.

Have I learned from this near-disastrous mistake? I hope so.

We are planning to open our fourth overseas office in India at the end of this year.

Lots of preparatory work has been done. We have even written a book for the Indian market.

But the key planning document we've still to finalize – and we won't set a date to open until we have – is the new company's cash-flow forecast.

28 July 1991

Philip Kogan

Philip Kogan, 61, is chairman of Kogan Page, the business publisher. He began his career as an industrial physicist after graduating from Reading and London universities. After ten years in research and development he changed direction, and eventually became the publishing director of Cornmarket Press. Kogan Page was launched in 1967. In 1984 the company joined a Business Expansion Scheme with Lazards Capital Development Funds and last year repurchased the shares. Philip Kogan is chairman of the European Business Publishing Network.

It is the nature of publishing that one is beset by one's own mistakes the whole time. My firm is offered thousands of books each year and publishes a couple of hundred. Among that mound of rejects there will be some big 'uns that got away.

But it is on the financial side of my business, rather than the publishing side, that I see our most significant mistake. My biggest mistake was not taking seriously enough our investment fund's stated reason for wanting to inject money into the company. I started the company with a £2,000 loan, but what began as some kind of masochistic hobby became, after a few years, a serious full-time business, with qualified staff, holidays and company cars.

Strong on product, moderately profitable, but weak on financial management, we got to the stage some ten years ago where we thought that BES money, with the subsequent glory of a USM quotation, should be our next step forward. The BES schemes seemed to suit us perfectly. The shareholders would have to surrender part of their equity, but we would retain a good majority. The money coming in was free of interest and could not be whipped away, so the nightmare of a banker pulling the rug need never disturb our sleep. Even the prospect of a non-executive director, supplied by our merchant bank's investment arm, was welcome.

In those days of high tax rates, the BES schemes offered great advantages to the investor. But the assumption was that they would come out after the five years were up with a good capital gain.

Our mistake was to think that five years was a long time, and that the injection of a few hundred thousand pounds would, in itself, make us much more profitable and efficient.

We could not reasonably blame the investment fund for this misconception. They had said plainly at the time what their objectives were, and, rightly, did not keep on reminding us about it until the end of the five-year period was looming.

They were, on behalf of their investors, bound into an equity holding in which they had limited scope for action with regard to disposals, while we, who had at that time under-performed – making adequate but unspectacular profits – were anxious to see them out.

So the big mistake had been not thinking about an exit, years aheads, in the likely event of things not going as planned. We had not performed well enough for a USM quotation, and we had to resist pressure to sell out. In the event, we took various management actions that we should have taken years earlier.

As a result, our figures soon looked good enough for our ordinary bankers to offer us a loan to repurchase the shares. But, in fact, to have done this would have been to follow a mistake with a catastrophe, in view of what subsequently happened to interest rates and market conditions generally. Fortunately, we were able to take another course of action. We sold some peripheral publishing assets in a good market at a good price, and this provided the capital we needed to repurchase.

Now we are fully independent and profitable. But we shall not easily forget those anxious months, locked in unhappy wedlock.

The moral? To quote our erstwhile merchant banker colleague: 'Never enter the yellow box unless you are sure that the exit is clear.'

1 September 1991

Janet Reger

Janet Reger, 55, is chairman of Designs by Janet Reger. She attended Leicester College of Art and spent ten years as a freelance designer before starting her lingerie business in 1967 with her husband Peter. Initially they operated from the dining-room of their home in Paddington, but within ten years owned a factory in Derbyshire and shops in Bond Street and Beauchamp Place. In 1983, she was forced into liquidation, but started again and today also designs swimwear and household textiles. Her autobiography, *Janet Reger: Her Story*, is published by Chapmans.

My biggest mistake was taking on too many financial commitments within a short space of time. In 1974, the business was flourishing and we increased our productivity by buying a factory. Just a few months later we took a small loan to buy the shop in Beauchamp Place.

We managed to pay for the factory in just two years, and the shop was so successful that we decided to look for another one in the Bond Street area. We found one in Brook Street at a price we could afford, and moved our design department into the basement. This shop was very successful too. By 1976 we had a big mail order business and countless customers buying for retail outlets around the world. The office space in Beauchamp Place had become rather cramped and we needed to take on more staff, so my husband started looking for somewhere else.

One day he came dashing round to Brook Street in great excitement to tell me he'd found wonderful offices in Bond Street. Underneath was a shop which had that look of 'I'm going to close any minute', and the agent said it was about to come on the market. The rent was £25,000 a year, which my husband felt was reasonable, though it was far more than the £7,000 we were paying for Brook Street.

We'd only been there for a year, but we decided to close it and move round the corner to what was a busier and more prestigious street. Bond Street being Bond Street, we wanted to make the shop look wonderfully elegant, so for the first time in our lives we started doing things we couldn't afford to do.

I had designed the previous shops myself, but this time we got an interior decorator. We were very extravagant – the wallpaper was made of hand-painted silk – and we opened with a great cocktail party and all the usual razzmatazz.

Up until then, we'd always borrowed small sums which we were able to pay back in two or three years. But Bond Street took us into a new realm of borrowing. Instead of being able to pay it back quite easily, we were beginning to rely on high projections.

For the first two years we did very well, then at the end of the 1970s we were hit by the recession. We had borrowed the money when interest rates were around 8 per cent, and by the early 1980s they had more than doubled.

Meanwhile, there had been rent reviews, so the Bond Street shop which had originally cost around £50,000 a year, including rates, suddenly cost £80,000.

We were having to pay out more and more, but our turnover wasn't increasing, because of recession. That was the beginning of our troubles. We tried various ways of increasing our turnover, but they all cost more money. So we made a series of mistakes trying to make up for the first mistake, which was buying the lease on Bond Street. If we had stayed in low-rent, low-rate premises, I have no doubt we would have survived.

It's very hard to see how the future is going to develop when you do these things. We had opened a factory in Derbyshire and two shops within the space of a year. To take on a further financial project was just too much, and we went into liquidation.

Next time round I made sure we didn't expand too fast. Today we have one shop in Beauchamp Place, another in the City, and our products are sold all over the country through licensees.

22 December 1991

John Ebenezer

John Ebenezer, 53, is managing director of the MCL Group, a medium-sized, diversified company in the motor industry which has been highly profitable since 1975. Its turnover for 1991 was £257m. Chairman of Mazda Cars (UK), as well as several other subsidiaries in the group, Ebenezer began his career in the motor industry in 1968 when he joined Volkswagen (GB) as chief accountant. He was appointed finance director the following year, but left in 1972 to buy into a small company importing two makes of car. It was the genesis of MCL.

Perhaps my biggest mistake was selling my 10 per cent holding in the MCL Group in 1975. If I had held on to it, I would be an extremely wealthy man. For the group now has a net worth of £40m and has declared dividends of £36m since 1975. But, of course, that thought is with the benefit of hindsight. At the time, it seemed the wise and prudent thing to do.

In 1972, I had left Volkswagen (GB) along with two fellow directors, to join with them in using borrowed money to buy Industria London Ltd, the forerunner of MCL. The company had the UK concession to import and distribute Mazda cars from Japan and the Wartburg from East Germany.

It soon became clear that the Wartburg was unlikely to do well in the UK, as it didn't measure up to the strengthened exhaust emission standards. Mazda was clearly the better bet, so we changed the name of the company to Mazda Car Imports. Later that year the MCL Group was formed.

But at the end of 1972, we still weren't doing well. It was worse still in 1973, when the oil crisis hit us especially hard. At that time, many Mazdas had rotary engines, which were notoriously thirsty.

TKM, a well-known player in the motor industry and recently acquired by the Inchcape Group, nevertheless bought an initial stake in the company from three of my fellow directors. And one of Japan's biggest trading houses, C Itoh, was also in the wings, expressing a strong interest in acquiring a stake in MCL.

But when you get big companies buying into little companies, it is wise, as a small shareholder, to prepare an exit for yourself. In 1974, with losses for the previous year already on the cards, I had to give a personal guarantee for a £2m shipment of Mazdas to the UK. I then decided I should sell my shareholding in the company as soon as the time was ripe. Lengthy and tortuous negotiations followed with C Itoh, which eventually acquired a 40 per cent stake in our loss-making company. It has since raised this to 60 per cent, making it the largest shareholder.

It required a great deal of vision to have confidence in a loss-maker. But at that time, C Itoh was better placed than me to know the strengths of the Japanese car industry. What's more, it was in a position to invest in the business and stand any losses in the meantime.

By 1975, I felt the time had come to sell, as the company was now in profit. I had no free cash. I had two young children. And I was still paying interest on the big loan I had taken out to buy my holding. So I sold out to C Itoh, making a healthy profit out of the deal.

It may have been my biggest mistake, for my stake would now be worth about £3m. But I am not saying it was a bad decision to take a profit out of the business, and I certainly have no bitter regrets about it. Money isn't everything.

Selling my stake was not an act of desertion. My personal shareholding was only a small part of my commitment to the company. I chose to stick with MCL and I was retained as managing director.

It has truly been a great fulfilment to build a team, now 400-strong, in a people-orientated company with a distinctive philosophy, where there is no 'them and us'.

What's more, the owners leave me free to run the company, which is still expanding despite the current difficulties of the motor industry.

5 January 1992

Peter Boizot

Peter Boizot, MBE, 62, is chairman and managing director of PizzaExpress, and proprietor of Kettners and Pizza on the Park. Previous jobs included being captain of a cargo ship and running a souvenir barrow in Rome. In 1965, he founded PizzaExpress; today there are 70 restaurants in the group, 55 of which are franchised. The turnover is £40m. He is vice-chairman of the Westminster Chamber of Commerce, founder and director of the Soho Jazz Festival, chairman of the Soho Restaurateurs Association, and a former Liberal candidate for Peterborough.

My biggest mistake was allowing my bank manager and one or two middle-of-the-road advisers to dissuade me from trying to buy the freeholds on two of my restaurants.

In the late 1970s, Soho was full of sex shops and in a state of general decline. Thus I was able to buy the lease on Kettners for £75,000 in 1980 and my rent was £55,000.

When De Vere Hotels decided to auction the freehold in 1984, their managing director advised me against buying it, saying I was better off paying rent. Accordingly, I didn't push very hard to raise the money.

I did ring the Midland Bank – with whom I've never had a very happy relationship – and ask if they'd help me buy it for around £700,000. They said no.

I should have gone to my friends in the City. My business at PizzaExpress was very profitable, and I could have put a package together. My mistake was to stand back and think: 'Well, nobody's encouraging me to fight for it.' On the day of the sale, there was one bid for £1.7m, which resulted in Paul Raymond owning half of the block. Immediately after, I was due for my first rent review. It went up to £90,000.

In 1990, when the next review came up, he wanted £400,000 a year. How was I supposed to cope with an extra £310,000 a year for a restaurant selling inexpensive food at around £10 a head?

It wasn't Paul Raymond's fault; he was being advised by a firm of estate agents and behaved like any other businessman. His attitude was: 'Tough. If you want to stay here, you've got to pay.'

But he didn't take into account that, over ten years, I had invested a lot of money in the place and had suffered great losses while building the business up. After battling against the system, we finally settled at £235,000 . . . £2,800 a week more than I was paying already.

I made the same mistake with Pizza on the Park. I took it on in 1976, but in 1985 the place was closed down for redevelopment. I put up a tremendous fight to stop it from being demolished and succeeded by bringing in Canada Life, who bought it for £1.4m.

Again, if I had tried, I could probably have raised funding to enable me and my consortium to buy the building and keep the restaurant without having to undergo colossal rent increases. In 1985, it was £15,000 a year, but after redevelopment the rent went up to £86,000 plus service charges. Five years later, they were asking £260,000.

Had I been the owner, I wouldn't have been saddled with these constant battles against estate agents, experts and others who take up so much of a businessman's time and money. With a little bit more effort, I could probably have bought both Kettners and Pizza on the Park. But instead, I listened to the advice of people who didn't have an entrepreneurial spirit, and I have kicked myself many times since.

If you have a hunch, you shouldn't listen to a safety-first bank manager; you should listen to people who are dynamic. I was prepared to take the risk; I was prepared to fight and make it work. But trying to get that belief across to funding institutions is often quite difficult.

It has certainly been a very expensive mistake, but it has made me realize that something must be done in this country about changing the system of commercial rent increases. Perhaps we can adopt some of the European practices; shorter leases, turnover rents, or increases that are indexed.

19 January 1992

Roger Young

Roger Young, 52, the new director-general of the British Institute of Management, has had a career centred on merchant and investment banking. He started with Drayton Group as an analyst, became an investment manager at an early age, then moved on to Imperial Tobacco and Robert Fleming. After executive directorships at Henry Ansbacher and Touche Remnant, he became chief executive of Bank Julius Baer, London, and later took on the same role at the March Group. He has held many non-executive appointments in private and quoted companies.

My biggest mistake so far – though it's difficult to choose from among the many I've made over the years – was also one of my first. That makes it memorable, and it taught me a valuable lesson.

In 1961, as a trainee in the corporate finance department at Drayton Group, I was helping out on a rights issue for Consolidated Gold Fields of South Africa, whose shares were quoted in both London and Johannesburg. We spent many evenings working late into the night on the preparation of the prospectus, which was to be used to raise additional finance. I therefore became intimately acquainted with the company's affairs, and it became clear to me that investment in machinery for existing and new mining projects would unlock a lot of latent potential.

Profits would go up, and once analysts realized this, so would the share price. Of course, even in those days, before insider trading rules had reached the statute book, there were ethical restrictions on buying quoted shares until price-sensitive information became public knowledge – so I did nothing until the official announcement.

When the announcement came, the shares were standing at five shillings and the nil-paid rights opened at around two pence – 1p in today's money. I immediately bought tens of thousands of them through an accommodating stockbroker who didn't require immediate settlement. This was just as well, as I had few liquid assets to support the purchases. Nevertheless, I was certain I could sell the shares at a large profit before I needed to find any money to pay for them.

Sure enough, as investors realized the potential, the shares rose. They reached six shillings, up 20 per cent, and the nil-paid rights I had bought quadrupled. On an 'investment' of around £2,500, I was looking at a profit of £7,500 or so – enough for a nice detached house in those days.

Clearly, a celebration was called for. I bought an enormous cigar, which I lit after lunch and finished when I was about to leave the office. The wireless the next morning was full of the news of South Africa's secession from the Commonwealth, a bolt from the blue that surprised the world. It shook the London Stock Exchange and shares in ConsGold fell back below their initial five shillings mark. Overnight, my nil-paid rights had become worthless. I still had to pay for them, though – without any prospect of gain and with money I didn't have to hand.

I had to sell all my realizable assets, including the National Savings Certificates given to me over the years by my parents, uncles and aunts. I felt terrible, particularly knowing of the sacrifices that many had made on my behalf. But the episode did bring home one of life's most important lessons: never bet more than you can afford to lose, even on a supposed racing certainty.

One should always look at what the maximum downside of a deal might be. Simply asking, 'What could we lose if something totally unexpected happened?' is vital – it has saved me from disaster on a number of occasions.

Fortunately, it has not stopped me from trying to succeed – or from making more mistakes. But I've always avoided open-ended commitments, or risks where I can't evaluate the maximum downside. I never became a Name at Lloyd's, for example. 'What if?' analyses are fine, but never think you can see all the angles.

5 April 1992

Part Four

Miscellaneous Mistakes

Just as some mistakes could be said to span all the categories chosen for this collection, others do not happily fit into any. But this problem of classification does not mean they are without value or interest.

For instance, not everybody gets the chance to choose their nationality. But former British Rail chairman Sir Peter Parker did – and feels he fluffed it. Clearly influenced by his time at BR, he envies the French – among whom he could now count himself on the grounds that he was born in Dunkirk – their approach to infrastructure, and particularly railways.

Digital Equipment's Geoff Shingles' mistake was almost as basic. He launched himself full of enthusiasm into the wrong career. Fortunately for him, he realized early enough that he was more suited to dealing with people than being an engineer and was able to make the change. But he learned that 'enthusiasm is no substitute for genius'.

And a genius must be the last thing that Portman Building Society chief executive Ken Culley thought he was when he accidentally disqualified two of the longest-serving directors from membership of the board. The happy ending to this embarrassing episode, like that described by Brian MacMahon, suggests that – for all the cynicism – there are people in business with some understanding of human nature and a lot of compassion.

Geoff Shingles

Geoff Shingles, 52, is a vice-president of Digital Equipment Corporation and chairman and chief executive of its UK subsidiary. He graduated from Leeds University with a BSc in electrical engineering and went on to do a post-graduate course in computer studies. He began his career as a computer design engineer at Mullard Radio Valve Company, then at Elliott-Automation. In 1968 he became general manager of Digital's UK subsidiary. He was appointed vice-president of the corporation in 1981, and chairman and chief executive of the UK company in 1991.

My biggest mistake was launching myself into the wrong career. I left university full of enthusiasm, thinking I could become a great engineer, but it gradually began to dawn on me over a period of four years that in fact I was rather mediocre.

Certainly I had the energy and the ambition to be good, but I didn't have the talent or the skills. I was competent, but if I looked around me I could see as many as ten other people who were at least as good, if not better. Meanwhile, others were coming up with ideas and approaches that I wouldn't have thought of until hell freezes over.

It was not so much what I did wrong as what I simply didn't do. I realized that if I had any ambition to stand out, I was probably in the wrong job. By then I had discovered I had other talents that I hadn't valued before, which would probably be pretty useful in a commercial environment, namely getting on well with people and being able to solve their problems.

Solving problems doesn't mean you have to know all the answers, it just means you have to know someone who does. To me it was pretty obvious that I had to get a role in which I was dealing with people instead of things. In the three years I was with Elliott-Automation as a development engineer working on the design of computers, I was never once able to speak to my boss's boss. It was a very hierarchical company, and they just didn't seem interested in their employees. I didn't think it was a very good way of dealing with people, and I vowed that if I ever got into a position of responsibility, I would never treat anyone working for me like that.

When I joined Digital in 1965 there were only five of us, and I was keen to take anything they were offering because in a company that small everybody does a bit of everything. We were dealing directly with a broad range of customers and for me it was very liberating. The stable door was open and the horse was galloping around the field, having a ball.

My career really took off, and by the time I was 28, which seems a hell of a long while ago, I was, in effect, the managing director. There were a hundred people in the company then, and the turnover was just over £1m. Today the organization employs about 7,000 and our turnover is more than £800m, so it's moved along a bit.

As a result of my experience at Elliott-Automation, Digital has a very open-door policy. We spend a great deal of time and energy on communicating effectively, not just with those outside the company, but with those inside as well. We have a very flat management structure. If you need something done, you talk to the person who is best able to do the job, whether it's the managing director, an administrator, an engineer or a janitor.

The real fascination for me turned out to be not the design of the machines, but the way that they are used and the people who work with them. The fact is, whatever career you choose, you need more than just enthusiasm to be successful. Vital though it is, enthusiasm is no substitute for genius.

I'm just glad I realized fairly early on that I wasn't a genius and that I had to find a career in which I could use what talents I did have to good effect.

19 April 1992

Ken Culley

Ken Culley, 49, is chief executive of the Portman Building Society. He started his career with the Cheshire Building Society in 1961, then worked for the Bradford & Bingley. In 1983 he became chief executive of the Ramsbury Building Society, which at the time employed 140 staff and had assets of £125m. A series of mergers then led to the creation of the Portman Building Society in 1990, and today that organization employs around a thousand people and has assets of more than £2.5bn. Mr Culley is a Fellow of the Chartered Building Societies Institute.

My big mistake was in 1984, when I misinterpreted the rules regarding the re-election of directors to the board. When I joined the Ramsbury Building Society, Sir Maurice Dorman, who was previously Governor-General of Malta, had just been appointed chairman, and during the course of the year we appointed three new non-executive directors. Each year, at the annual general meeting, all building societies are required to re-elect any new directors as well as a number of the original board.

Unfortunately, in my role as the new chief executive and secretary, I put forward only the directors who had been elected during the year. As a result, Sir Maurice and Stephen Hurd, brother of Foreign Secretary Douglas Hurd and the longest-serving director of the society, were automatically disqualified.

My error only became apparent at the AGM, when a member queried whether my interpretation was correct, as he thought we should also be re-electing part of the original board. I didn't think he could possibly be right, because I had consulted a colleague who confirmed that what I had done was correct.

So we simply said we would take his point on board and come back to him. We then took advice from our solicitors, but they weren't absolutely sure about the interpretation either. So we went to leading counsel, who confirmed that this man in the audience, from a firm of accountants in the town, was right. We therefore had to do something to get Sir Maurice and Stephen Hurd back on the board.

Meanwhile, I had to break the news to them that our worst fears had been realized. Sir Maurice is a wonderful man whom I hold in the highest possible regard. However, I had only been with the Ramsbury for nine months, and it did cross my mind that they might wonder about this idiot from the North who had come down and decimated the board in a single stroke.

In the event, I needn't have worried about their reactions. Sir Maurice just said: 'Well, Ken, we've got to put it right. Let's do it as quickly as we possibly can.' Stephen Hurd's response was much the same. They couldn't serve as directors from the date of the AGM until they were re-elected, and for that we had to get more than 100 members to sign a proposal for a special meeting.

It took from April until October for Sir Maurice and Stephen Hurd to be reinstated. Meanwhile, having ceased to be directors, they had also ceased to be paid.

I was acutely embarrassed. I had got rid of the chairman and the longest-serving director, done them out of their fees for six months, and incurred leading counsel's fees for the society to go through the process of getting them re-elected. The only good thing to come out of it was that it gave me a much better insight into the characteristics of the board than anything else I could have done.

I started to learn how they thought, how they would behave in a crisis, whether they would support me when I dropped clangers, and so on. In fact, they were just marvellous. They really were incredibly supportive. But it certainly taught me a lesson I have never forgotten: in any circumstances where there is a possibility of misinterpretations, you must always get the best legal advice. In the long term, it can save a lot of costs and embarrassment.

3 May 1992

Brian Macmahon

Brian MacMahon, 54, is group pensions executive of BET and chairman of the National Association of Pension Funds. He was educated at Terenure College, Dublin, then in 1955 joined Irish Pensions Trust. In 1973 he left to join Allied Breweries in Bristol, and in 1982 became group pensions executive of BET. He was elected to the NAPF Council in 1983, and has been chairman of the public relations and parliamentary committees. He is a fellow of the Pensions Management Institute and a member of the Council of the Occupational Pensions Advisory Service.

My biggest mistake was just over 30 years ago, when I was working for Irish Pensions Trust. My role was to administer pension schemes for companies. I suppose everybody at some stage or other has an in-tray containing things that you've got to get around to but somehow haven't. In most cases you get away with it, though you might be a day or two late. But in this instance I had failed to renew a very important client's life assurance policy. The renewal date was 1 September and I was about ten days late.

It was a Friday; I was getting married the following day and going on honeymoon for a fortnight. Just as I was about to leave, I was called into my boss's office. He said a very sad event had taken place: the managing director of my client had died. I knew straight away that I hadn't arranged the cover. I couldn't believe it. It was Murphy's Law that someone would die within ten days of the renewal date. First of all I went back to my office and checked whether by some miracle I had done it after all. But I hadn't: it was still sitting in my in-tray. I had to go back and say:'Look, I'm afraid there's been a terrible error.'

The man who had died should have been covered for £100,000. His widow was expecting to receive the money, and it just wouldn't be there. There was absolute panic. My bosses were very angry and naturally very concerned, because £100,000 was a lot of money in those days. But they were very good about it. They said: 'You can't change your arrangements. You go off, we'll sort it out, and we'll discuss your future when you come back.'

I was still relatively young and I really didn't know what was going to happen. The sum was so vast, there was just no way I could have paid it back, even if they docked my pay by a fiver a week for life. I had fallen in love with pensions as a career. I liked the human element of it, the provision of benefits. I was really afraid that I was going to be dismissed, and for the worst possible reason . . . I wasn't reliable. To have that hanging over my head for ever after would have been terrible. Two things you look for in a pensions administrator are reliability and trustworthiness.

But on my return, I went straight into the boss's office to find it had all been dealt with. Their attitude was: 'We're sure it won't happen again now you realize the consequences.' And that's all that was said. I learnt a lot from this ghastly experience. One lesson is that when you're dealing with other people's livelihoods, you've got to do everything on time in order to make sure that the benefits you have promised are there. It has also made me very sensitive in my dealings with staff. It is part of management to recognize that anyone can make a mistake, and I have always appreciated the loyalty shown to me by my bosses.

They never gave the slightest indication to the clients that there was anything amiss, so when I resumed my normal duties, all they had was appreciation for the fact that the widow of a senior executive had been looked after.

It really taught me a lot about crisis management. You must show absolute loyalty to your employees, stand by your obligations and solve the crisis with the minimum of fuss. But that experience still lives with me. It was a very scary time.

28 June 1992

Tony Fraher

Tony Fraher, 40, was born in Dublin. He trained as an accountant and joined the investment division of Bank of Ireland in 1971. In 1977 he joined Allied Irish Investment Bank as an investment manager, specializing in charity funds. He was made a board director and moved to London in 1983 to set up a UK investment division. In 1987 Morgan Grenfell asked him to set up its unit trust and retail division. He is a board director of Morgan Grenfell Asset Management and managing director of Morgan Grenfell Unit Trust Managers.

It's very important in business to research properly and do your homework. Yet you can be as prepared as you like and there's always going to be that one little item that you overlook – and it's rarely to do with business. This was the reason I made my biggest mistake.

It happened in 1980, when I was working as an investment manager with the Allied Irish Investment Bank in Dublin. I had developed a specialization in managing the investment of charitable funds. Before that the charities had just had their funds on deposit with the banks and I'd seen a market gap. Most of the charities were religious and I had found that I was acceptable to all denominations and charities both north and south of the border, partly because of my name. Gilbert Anthony Fraher is not an Irish name and while Gilbert Fraher is very much a non-Roman Catholic name, Tony was more acceptable to the Catholics. I never told anyone my religion.

In three years, from 1977 to 1980, I had cornered 83 per cent of the total market worth £300–£400m. Naturally our competitors were very keen to get in, but by 1980 I had most of the bishops, nuns, priests, Presbyterians, Christian Scientists – you name them.

But my moment of glory came with one bishop that I hadn't been able to move. For years I had researched and worked on him, and eventually he agreed to see me. A colleague and I were bid to arrive at his home in the deep rural south of Ireland at a quarter to twelve one day.

Now I prided myself on the amount of homework and research I always did on every client. But I should have realized that the bishop was also doing his homework. He was used to talking to his local bank manager and here were these investment types coming down to see him.

Not only that, but he was suspicious of my name – and of my colleague who had a very Jewish name, although in fact he was a very devout Roman Catholic.

We arrived at 11.45 and were given a glass of sherry. We sat, going through the pleasantries before getting down to the serious stuff when, at noon, the Angelus bell rang from the cathedral.

And something happened that had never happened before. For all my great preparation I had completely overlooked it. The Bishop said, 'Let us pray'. He stood up, and in the shock so did I, knocking over the table, the sherry, my cigarette and the ashtray on his carpet. But he kept going.

My colleague was fine. He knew all the words and I mumbled my way through the first one. The Angelus is the same prayer repeated three times, so by the second time I was getting the hang of it and could almost synchronize my words.

But the Bishop had spotted all of this, and when it came to the third one he threw me a complete wobbler. He changed to Gaelic and that totally destroyed me. I just looked at him, then I looked at my colleague and I thought, Oh dear.

All of this took about three minutes and wiped out three years of research and work. The meeting endured for a further ten frosty minutes whereupon we were informed that there was no interest in our services. Three days later we heard that our biggest competitor, who'd been looking to get a toe-hold in the market, had been appointed investment manager to this bishop. In Ireland Allied Irish Investment Bank still has a 63 per cent share of that market. But for the want of a Hail Mary I left a gap for a competitor.

2 September 1990

John Willan

John Willan, 48, is managing director of the London Philharmonic. After leaving Edinburgh University, he became a chartered accountant, but soon realized he would rather be in the music business. He took a another degree at Edinburgh and then joined EMI, where he became a classical record producer. He was promoted to manager of classic productions for EMI Music Worldwide. After twelve years with the company, he left in 1985 to run The London Philharmonic. In 1990, it became the resident orchestra at the Royal Festival Hall.

My biggest mistakes have always been made when I've acted on impulse. On more than one occasion, it has nearly cost me my job. But when I worked at EMI's Abbey Road studios, I learnt a lesson which I have never forgotten.

I was very fortunate that the boss at EMI was my old schoolmaster. Having changed career, I was very pleased to get the job. My training was spent sitting next to him in the control room watching, and within a very short space of time I was convinced I could do it better. On one occasion, when I was still terribly new, and very green, I was in charge of synchronizing the tea breaks between the London Philharmonic in Studio One, and a big band up in Studio Two.

It was absolutely impossible, because they kept deciding to go for another take. Dolly in the canteen could not cope with more than 50 people at once, but I could not explain that to Sir Adrian Boult. All he was interested in was the symphony. So I was rushing up and down stairs for about half an hour, trying to liaise with Alan, the assistant engineer, who was in a little vestibule off the control room.

There was a bit of banter building up, and at one point I tore upstairs and dashed into the studio, failing to notice that the red light was on and they were recording. I got some friendly abuse from Alan, and in response, I made to stab at the stop button on this huge 24-track machine to give him a fright. The trouble was, I actually hit the button. All the lights changed colour and it came to a grinding halt with a great metallic clunk.

I just died. I still remember the look on Alan's face. It was just extraordinary. His mouth was open, and he said: 'My God, what am I going to do?' And I ran. The engineer and producer still thought they were recording. They had spent three days trying to get it right, and as Alan was tapping them on the shoulder, they were saying: 'Great! We've got it this time.'

Meanwhile, I was back in the control room of Studio One. I was sitting there wondering what to do next – go back into accountancy, perhaps. Ten minutes later the door opened, and there was the producer of the session upstairs with a really hard look on his face. I panicked. He stood there for about 20 seconds, then just burst into laughter.

Somehow I managed to keep my job, but it taught me quite a lesson. When you're working, you do not mess about. It's uncharacteristic of me to be rash, because I'm the product of a public boarding school where you're taught not to blub when mummy leaves you on the doorstep. Any sort of emotional response gets subsumed, and as a result, I'm often told that in meetings nobody has any idea what I'm thinking. I do a lot of listening, and I generally talk quite late in the day. So when I do let my emotions out, I try to keep them in check.

Today, when I get angry or I want to do something really outrageous, I have to remind myself that I have an important responsibility. I expect everybody else to be professional, therefore I have to lead by example. You have to think before you leap.

Even after twelve years, whenever I go back to Abbey Road, people pull my leg about that mistake. And I have never played a practical joke since. Not one.

22 September 1991

Sir Peter Parker

Sir Peter Parker, 65, served as chairman of British Rail from 1976 to 1983. His activities now range from chairmanship of Rockware, to which he returned after his spell at BR, and the London School of Economics to trusteeship of Friends of the Earth. After serving with the army during the Second World War, he attended Oxford University. In 1951, he stood for Labour in Bedford. But he was also fascinated by management, and became chairman of Rockware before joining BR.

As chairman of British Railways, I sometimes wondered if I had made a great mistake more than 30 years before when I was an army lieutenant on the joint staff mission in Washington. I turned 21 on 30 August 1945, and I was given the chance of taking French nationality. I turned it down, but later, when I saw how handsomely the French looked after their railways, I wondered if I had been wise.

I could have been French simply because I was born in Dunkirk, where my father worked as an engineer for a French refrigerating firm. I lived there until 1931, when my father was made redundant and we took a slow boat to China – but that is another story. As it was, by the time I was given the chance to choose my passport, I had spent two years in the British Army in India, Burma and Japan, so I said no without thinking much about it.

I don't speak French all that well now, although I can understand it: my elder brother, who didn't leave France until he was fourteen (and was killed in the war), was bilingual. But although I am a free marketeer – there is nothing so boring as thinking you can live by plans – I admire the way the French put infrastructure at the centre of their lives.

De Gaulle sorted out the basic principles of transport in Paris, integrating where it was needed, while London is now strangling itself to death because the British took such a fragmented approach. We built airports without even considering railways, and now we are regretting it bitterly.

The French have always been particularly keen on railways, taking immense pride in them and treating them as part of the quality of life. Five years is an eternity for a politician but a short time for a railwayman:

if you are going to do something serious you have to take a long-term view, and the French understand that. In his elegant swansong, my successor, Sir Robert Reid, could not avoid once again having to remind government to take the long view.

When I joined British Rail, I worked with French railways to revive the Channel tunnel project. I set up a near-secret study with SNCF to look at the possibility of a fully commercial single railway tunnel: my speech proposing it was co-ordinated with one made by my French counterpart. I think we set the debate going again, even though the Labour government of the time (it was 1978) wasn't keen on a tunnel. I've always taken the view that the tunnel is a nation-to-nation – or rather nations-to-nations – thing, and needs a partnership of the private, public and government sectors.

Whether I would rather have stayed and grown up in France is a more difficult question. I would have gone through the hell of the Occupation and would have missed the wonderful eccentricities of the British and their politics. But I do like the way the French have a marvellously uninhibited and unstuffy attitude. I like their sense of proportion and particularly where art is placed in society. It is marvellous having a president who takes a keen interest in the country's architecture.

There is the other interesting question of whether I could ever have become chairman of French Railways. When I joined BR, I don't think there was an engineer on the board. At SNCF, seventeen of the top 20 people were engineers – and my degree is in history. You can see how that gives the French an advantage in the balance of power when foreign and British companies come together: most times the foreign partner takes the lead.

Other people have said the same thing, but the real battle in Britain is to get the status of engineering where it should be: otherwise we will go on marginalizing ourselves.

18 March 1990

Howard Hodgson

Howard Hodgson, 40, is an unlikely looking fifth-generation funeral director. He bought Hodgson Holdings for £14,000 from his father in 1975, when it was conducting 400 funerals a year. Since then he has taken the company public, and last year merged with Kenyon Securities (another quoted UK undertaker) and Pompes Funèbres of France. PFG Hodgson Kenyon now manages more than 70,000 funerals a year and has diversified into other businesses, including financial services and car hire.

My biggest mistake was not spotting a fundamental error in a brochure describing a new product called Dignity in Destiny. It led to confusion in the City and the Press, which then criticized Hodgson Holdings for being too commercial about pre-paid funerals and raking off an excessive profit by calling it a service charge.

For several years people had been coming into our funeral homes or branch offices and asking to arrange and pay for their funeral in advance. We decided to organize ourselves properly so that we could meet this public demand.

We brought together a team of financial and legal experts, along with the charity Help the Aged to represent the interests of the customer. Over the next year we had so many drafting meetings it was incredible, and we took immense care over the writing of Dignity in Destiny, which was to offer customers a choice of funerals which could be paid for in advance. Rather than taking the revenue on sales straight into Hodgson Holdings, we decided to set up a limited company called Dignity in Destiny with its own sales team.

We limited Dignity in Destiny to drawing off a maximum 25 per cent of the revenue to pay for its setting up, marketing and other overheads. The rest would go into a Gartmore-managed investment fund. We felt that, as well as being a safe way of providing security for the future cost of funerals, this would also inspire consumer confidence. It seemed a sensible way to handle the income while we were able to sell a product at a unit price with no membership fees or management fees bolted on.

When we launched Dignity in Destiny in February 1989 (Help the Aged took a 5 per cent share and B & C ventures a further 20 per cent) it was well received. But then, three weeks later, Schroder Securities, the broker, brought out a survey which criticized Hodgson Holdings for taking a 25 per cent service fee on the product, remarking that this was excessive. The comments were picked up by *The Times*.

We'd had three years of good press so this was quite a foreign thing for us. And everyone was furious. We thought it was so unfair, because we were not taking a 25 per cent service fee.

However, when the steam had stopped coming out of my ears I said to the team, 'You know, I think this is our fault. Look at what the brochure says.' Sure enough, we hadn't worded it properly. The launch brochure summed up Dignity in Destiny in eight bullet points. And one of them clearly stated 'a separate trust fund for your payments (less the initial service charge) has been established by Dignity in Destiny'. In the terms and conditions it said that up to 25 per cent could be drawn down for the company's use, which was how the analyst had arrived at a 25 per cent service fee.

We just hadn't realized that what we'd written implied that we were setting up a trust fund for the funeral fees and charging a separate management fee for us on top. We'd never thought to pull in anyone to look at it with a fresh eye who might have spotted this.

I was very depressed after all of this – I saw it as a tremendous soiling of something very good. What they had taken our brochure to mean was inherently wrong and questioned our professional integrity. I thought we'd have to stand up for the next ten years and explain that, no, that wasn't it at all. But I was amazed to realize later that it didn't do any damage at all. We explained what we'd intended to the analyst, reworded the brochure and a BBC2 programme broadcast in June about the developing of Dignity in Destiny was favourable. We started writing contracts in July, and in nine months we've sold nearly 3,000 pre-arranged funerals.

8 April 1990

Index of names